Ichthus

Ichthus

Jesus Christ, God's Son, the Saviour

Sinclair B. Ferguson
&
Derek W. H. Thomas

THE BANNER OF TRUTH TRUST

THE BANNER OF TRUTH TRUST
3 Murrayfield Road, Edinburgh EH12 6EL, UK
P.O. Box 621, Carlisle, PA 17013, USA

❊

© Sinclair B. Ferguson & Derek W. H. Thomas 2015

ISBN:
PRINT: 978-1-84871-620-9
EPUB: 978-1-84871-621-6
KINDLE: 978-1-84871-622-3

❊

Typeset in 11/13 pt Adobe Garamond Pro at
The Banner of Truth Trust, Edinburgh

Printed in the USA by
Versa Press, Inc.,
East Peoria, IL

To

John Richard de Witt

Predecessor and Friend

and

In memory of

Jane Epps de Witt

Encourager

Contents

Introduction ix

1. The Manger – *Incarnation* 3
2. The River – *Baptism* 21
3. The Wilderness – *Temptation* 35
4. The Mountain – *Transfiguration* 55
5. The Garden – *Decision* 67
6. The Cross – *Passion* 83
7. The Tomb – *Resurrection* 105
8. The Throne – *Ascension* 129
9. The Return – *Coming* 145

Introduction

ICHTHUS. It may seem a very strange title for a book, but the chances are you have seen an *ichthus*. It is the Greek word for a fish. You have probably seen an *ichthus* on the rear bumper of an automobile, or as a lapel badge, or perhaps on a poster.

It is an ancient symbol for the Christian faith – a simple sign, perhaps traced on the ground by a stick, or doodled somewhere as an indication that the person drawing it was a Christian.

How did this symbol come to be associated with Christianity? Perhaps because four of Jesus' first disciples were fishermen? Perhaps. But undoubtedly because the five Greek letters which spell *ichthus* are also the first letters of a simple confession of faith: 'Jesus Christ is the Son of God and Saviour.' To draw the sign was to say wordlessly: 'I am a Christian.'

To be a Christian, according to the New Testament is 'to know Christ'.[1] But how? In fact the only reliable sources we have for knowing anything about him are to be found in the New Testament.

Our aim, then, in these pages is to explore what the New Testament has to say about the identity of Jesus. We plan to do this by looking at nine critical moments in his life and ministry. These form a series of dots on the pages of the New Testament which, when joined up, give us a portrait of Jesus and help us to see the significance of who he is and what he has done. That, in turn, is what helps us to trust him in exactly the same way the first Christians did, as our Saviour and Lord.

Ichthus is a book for everyone and anyone. We hope it will be a help to believers because of what it says about our Master. But we also hope

[1] Philippians 3:8.

it will be read by those who are not – or perhaps not yet – believers, because all of us should at least know who Jesus was and what claims he made. It would be less than honest to reject him without knowing anything about him.[1]

Like all books *Ichthus* has a 'back story'. Its two authors have known each other and been friends for forty years. Our lives have run in parallel lines. We are both Celts (one Welsh, the other Scottish); we have both been ministers in the United Kingdom (one in Northern Ireland, the other in Scotland); we have both experienced transplantation to the USA to teach in theological seminaries (one in Jackson, Mississippi and Atlanta, the other in Philadelphia and Dallas).

Throughout those decades we have met, corresponded, spoken together at various conferences, and supported and encouraged each other in different ways. But for two memorable years, from 2011 to 2013, we had the unexpected privilege of serving the same congregation together, First Presbyterian Church, Columbia, South Carolina. For one of us this came in his final two years, for the other in the opening two years of our ministry to a congregation that wonderfully embraced us and made us part of its life.

All of which leads to this book. In the final weeks of our work together we wanted to express two things: continuity on the one hand, and what was central to our ministries on the other. And so we brought to the church a series of expositions on the high points in Christ's life and ministry. The substance of these expositions we have now transposed from one medium (words spoken to people we know and love well) to the very different medium of a book (words written for many people we do not know). In one sense *Ichthus* is the book that lay behind the expositions.

We are indebted to those who have helped to make this book possible.

We are especially grateful to Dr Patricia Wilson for transcribing the original messages for us.

To our wives Dorothy and Rosemary we continue to owe an

---

[1] *Ichthus* does not tell the whole story of Jesus' life and ministry. But we hope that its focus on its 'high points' will help to set the whole of his work in its proper context.

unrepayable debt for all they do as our supporters and best friends.

To the congregation of First Presbyterian Church in Columbia we owe a double debt, first for giving each of us the privilege of serving as their senior minister, and for the very special privilege of serving together for a memorable season in our lives.

Most Sunday evenings, as we stood in the pulpit of First Presbyterian Church, looking out on its full auditorium of eager worshippers and listeners, we could spot our distinguished predecessor Dr John Richard de Witt seated in his usual place in the congregation. Jesus said: 'One sows and another reaps' and 'the sower and the reaper rejoice together' (John 4:37-38). This has been our experience as we have followed him in pastoral ministry. For that reason it is to Dr de Witt, and in memory of his wife Jane, that these pages are dedicated.

SINCLAIR B. FERGUSON
DEREK W. H. THOMAS
July 2015

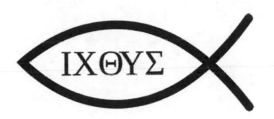

'ΙΧΘΥΣ

'Ιησοῦς	=	Jesus
Χριστός	=	Christ
Θεοῦ	=	God's
Υἱός	=	Son
Σωτήρ	=	Saviour

1. The Manger – *Incarnation*

Who is He, in yonder stall,
At whose feet the shepherds fall?

'Tis the Lord! O wondrous story!
'Tis the Lord! the King of glory!
At His feet we humbly fall;
Crown Him, Crown Him Lord of all.

John 1:1-18[1]

In the beginning was the Word, and the Word was with God, and the Word was God. [2] He was in the beginning with God. [3] All things were made through him, and without him was not any thing made that was made. [4] In him was life, and the life was the light of men. [5] The light shines in the darkness, and the darkness has not overcome it.

[6] There was a man sent from God, whose name was John. [7] He came as a witness, to bear witness about the light, that all might believe through him. [8] He was not the light, but came to bear witness about the light.

[9] The true light, which gives light to everyone, was coming into the world. [10] He was in the world, and the world was made through him, yet the world did not know him. [11] He came to his own and his own people did not receive him. [12] But to all who did receive him, who believed in his name, he gave the right to become children of God, [13] who were born, not of blood nor of the will of the flesh nor of the will of man, but of God.

[14] And the Word became flesh and dwelt among us, and we have seen his glory, glory as of the only Son from the Father, full of grace and truth. [15] (John bore witness about him, and cried out, 'This was he of whom I said, "He who comes after me ranks before me, because he was before me."') [16] For from his fullness we have all received, grace upon grace. [17] For the law was given through Moses; grace and truth came through Jesus Christ. [18] No one has ever seen God; the only God, who is at the Father's side, he has made him known.

---

[1] It will be helpful for readers to take a few minutes to familiarize themselves with the passages that precede each of the chapters of *Ichthus* and that provide the New Testament's account of each of the events in Christ's life on which these chapters are based.

ICHTHUS: Jesus is the Christ, the Son of God, and the Saviour. Each of these aspects of Jesus' identity is either mentioned or alluded to in the majestic opening overture to *The Gospel according to John*. Whoever first thought of the word for fish as a mnemonic for the person and work of Christ certainly understood the fourth Gospel.

By common consent John is the Gospel writer who gives us the grandest and largest vision of what it meant for the Son of God to come into this world.

Each of the Gospel writers had his own particular audience for which he recorded his story and message about Jesus. Together they harmonize into a remarkable portrait. At the same time there is something about John's Gospel that sets it apart. It seems to bring us right inside Jesus' mind and heart. And as its story unfolds we find ourselves drawn deeper and deeper into an appreciation of him. John Calvin put it memorably. 'Since all the Gospel writers had the same object, to show Christ, the first three exhibit His body, if I may be permitted to put it like that, but John shows His soul.'[1]

John's literary skills become immediately obvious in his Prologue. If we know anything about the gospel story we immediately realize that 'The Word' about which he writes is Jesus. Yet he does not actually identify him by name until almost at the end – in verse 17. Then he confirms our suspicions: he has been speaking about Jesus all along.

We tend to hear this part of John's Gospel only at Christmas time. But there are good reasons to think about 'the Christmas message' all the year round! In fact *think* is exactly what we need to try to do when we read these particular words, because John is taking us places we are not sure we can reach. But it is this experience – discovering the sheer profundity of who Jesus is and what he has done – that brings

[1] John Calvin, *The Gospel according to St John*, tr. T. H. L. Parker, eds. D. W. and T. F. Torrance (Edinburgh: Oliver and Boyd, 1959), vol. 1, 6.

a sense of awe and wonder into our hearts and minds. Then we begin to sing – as so many Christians have:

> To Him all majesty ascribe,
> And crown Him Lord of all.[1]

The Word

John describes Jesus as *the Word of God*: 'In the beginning was the Word.'

Why would he describe a *person* as a *word*? Perhaps because the Greek word *logos* ('word') expressed a common enough concept in antiquity. It denoted not only speech, but reason, the integrating element in the universe. Entire world-and-life views were built around the concept.

John, however, did not base his understanding of the term on the culture and philosophy of the secular world in which he lived, but on the Bible that he had studied.

The Word was God

The first thing we notice about John's description of Jesus as the Word is that he identifies him as someone with a divine nature.

Three of the Gospel authors wrote about the coming of Jesus. But they all have different starting places:

- Matthew begins with Abraham.
- Luke begins with the parents of John the Baptist.
- John begins in eternity.

John may well have known the other Gospels. He agrees with all they say. But he wants to take us back to an older, earlier, deeper and more mysterious starting place. He goes beyond Abraham, and even beyond Adam, to the very first words of the Hebrew Bible and to 'the beginning'.[2] He borrows language from the opening words of the Scriptures in order to help us understand who Jesus really is.

---

[1] From the hymn by Edward Perronet (1726–92) 'All hail the power of Jesus' Name.' Perronet's last words were 'Glory to God in the height of his divinity! Glory to God in the depth of his humanity! Glory to God in his all-sufficiency! Into his hands I commend my spirit.'

[2] See Genesis 1:1.

To say that Jesus is the Word of God is a neat summary of Genesis chapter 1. It tells us that he was heavily involved in bringing creation into being. You simply cannot miss that pulse-beat as you read it – especially if you read it the way it was originally intended: out loud. Again and again we are told: God spoke his word and things came into being.[1] Everything he spoke created something that was 'good', and ultimately the whole creation was *very* good. John is telling us: 'Jesus is that Word God spoke.' By him all things were created.

This is the claim of a man who knew Jesus intimately. At the Last Supper he sat near enough Jesus to be able to lean against him.[2] Intriguingly (and probably deliberately) he uses an almost identical expression on only one other occasion: to describe the relationship between the Word and God the Father: he is 'at the Father's side'.[3] The idea expresses close relationship.

So John's claim was not made by a stranger. No. John, who knew him as well as anybody did, believed Jesus was the Son of God come in the frailty and weakness of our flesh. His coming was not merely a birth; it was an *incarnation*.

At the same time John is helping us understand creation. That creative speech of God described in Genesis chapter 1 was not simply a sound. No, it was – and still is – a person! The entire created order has a personal, not an impersonal foundation. What brought it into being was not a temporal force but God's eternal Son.

This single statement – 'The Word was God' – has enormous consequences for the way we think about everything. It means our world is not a cosmic accident, the effect of 'chance'. It explains how it can be that something has come from nothing, and confirms that the personal did not emerge from that which is completely impersonal. Behind everything stands a person. We are not alone in the universe, imprisoned in a vast 'clockwork orange'. For in the very beginning was the Word.

This Word – says John – 'was God'. He was 'in the beginning'.

[1] See Genesis 1:3, 6, 9, 11, 14, 20, 24, and 26.
[2] John 13:23-25.
[3] John 1:18.

But more than that, he was there 'with God'. He was 'God with God'!

What can this mean?

To begin with it explains some of the otherwise inexplicable statements we find in the Old Testament. For example, later in Genesis chapter 1 we are told that while God brought everything else into being by 'speaking' his Word, there was a divine preamble to the creation of man and woman that destined them to be the apex of creation. He brought them into being as his image and in his likeness. Not only so, but he did it after a mysterious consultation with … the Word who was God: 'Let *us* make man …'[1]

The Word with God

John reflects this when he says that 'the Word was *with* God'.

The preposition 'with' translates the Greek word *pros*, which means 'towards'. The Word was not merely *with* God in a general sense, he was *towards* God. He gave himself to God. He was, as one commentator suggests, 'face to face with God'.

In the Old Testament the people were taught that no one can look at God and live. If staring at a solar eclipse can damage our sight, how much less able are we to gaze directly at the infinite glory of God who created the sun and governs every solar eclipse! But there is an exception: God's own Son can do this. Whatever else John may be saying here, he is stressing the intimacy in the relationship between God the Son and God the Father. They gaze on each other!

This is surely one of the most profound statements in the whole of the New Testament. How can we even begin to fathom it?

God has planted analogies into our lives to help us grasp realities that are beyond our full comprehension or explanation. In this way the New Testament teaches us that we can 'comprehend' the love of Christ although it 'surpasses knowledge'.[2] This is so because we were made as the image of God.[3] His life is reflected in miniature ways in our lives.

For example, God made man male and female. A man 'falls in love' with a woman. He experiences an intimacy with her that he

[1] Genesis 1:26.
[2] Ephesians 3:18-19.
[3] Genesis 1:26-28.

scarcely knew existed. He gives himself to her, and at the same time he discovers himself in and through her. Barriers disappear. He loves to look into her eyes, to be 'face to face' with her. He feels he could be satisfied for ever with her, in her, and by her.

What else can this be but a little glimpse, an intimation given to us by the heavenly Father, a hint and echo of what is perfectly, infinitely and eternally true in the relationship between the heavenly Father and his Son?

But now, having described the intimacy of this relationship, John takes us a breathtaking step further: the Word who was 'face to face' with God has come 'face to face' with us. He has entered into our world, and indeed into the reality of the human condition.

So John is making important claims about Jesus.

• He is a fully divine person.
• He was in the beginning.
• He was 'face to face' with God.

And then he adds, very simply: 'and the Word was God': 'In the beginning was the Word and the Word was with God, and *the Word was God*.'

Deity contested?

Occasionally we meet Jehovah's Witnesses – perhaps on our doorsteps, or in passing conversation on a train or bus. When they discover we are Christians, they may insist on telling us that these words in John chapter 1 have been badly, indeed erroneously, translated in our Bibles. Traditionally they have argued that John 1:1 does not describe Jesus as 'God' but only as 'a god' or as 'divine'. John did not mean what we think he did.

The characteristic argument here has been as follows: In the Greek text of John 1:1 there is no definite article ('the') before the word *theos* ('God'). Therefore *theos* here means 'a god' not 'God'.[1]

What should we think about this, especially since it is in fact true that in John 1:1 the word *theos* lacks the definite article?[2]

[1] *The New World Translation of the Holy Scriptures* (2013 revision) translates John 1:1: 'In the beginning was the Word, and the Word was with God, *and the Word was a god*' (emphasis added). A footnote reads: 'or was "divine".'

[2] In technical grammatical terms it is *anarthrous i.e.* lacking the definite article before the noun.

Several things:

• In the verses that follow the word *theos* appears without the definite article (in verse 6: 'There was a man sent from God'; and in verse 12: 'he gave the right to become children of God'). But clearly in both of these statements John refers to the one true and living God.

• In many languages, including Greek, a definite noun, especially if it expresses a title, can appear without the definite article ('the').

If, for example, we say in 2015 'Elizabeth is Queen of the United Kingdom' we mean exactly the same as if we had said 'Elizabeth is *the* Queen of the United Kingdom.' We do not mean that she is either one of several contemporaneous queens, or that she is anything less than truly and fully queen!

There is another example of an indefinite noun having this definite sense later in John chapter 1. Nathanael says to Jesus, 'You are the King (*basileus*) of Israel.'[1] There is no definite article before the word 'king' (here it would be the Greek '*ho*', which is the equivalent of 'the' in English). But the context makes it quite obvious that Nathanael means 'You are *the* King of Israel.' In fact Nathanael means that Jesus is the real and true king.

• The significance of a word is always determined by the context in which it appears, not merely by grammatical form. In the context of his Gospel John can mean only that 'the Word was (and is) God'. For he goes on to ascribe to the Word attributes and actions that in Scripture belong exclusively to God:

> All things were made through him.
>
> Without him was not anything made that was made.
>
> The world was made through him.
>
> He gave the right to become children of God.[2]

The Word does not belong to the order of created beings. He is uncreated. He is on the side of God, not on the side of creation. (This is why his incarnation is so astonishing). He has the authority to bring us into the family of God.

• The big picture in John's Gospel also underlines this. Jesus claims

[1] John 1:49.
[2] John 1:3, 10, 12.

unity with God the Father ('I and my Father are one'; – a statement immediately recognized to be blasphemy unless it were true[1]); 'whoever has seen me has seen the Father'.[2]

• The climax of the Gospel is found in Thomas's famous confession: 'My Lord and my God!'[3] Here even *The New World Translation* of the Jehovah's Witnesses has no option but to translate the Greek text this way (including a capital letter for 'God'!). This perfectly matches the way in which Christ is described in John 1:1.

• There is a further, technical reason for John's language. If he had used the definite article he could have given the impression that the Word was God in the sense that the Word is all God is. But in fact he was wanting to distinguish between God the Son (the Word) and God the Father.[4]

Deity known

What then is John saying? From the very beginning he wants readers of his Gospel to appreciate that the Lord Jesus is God as well as man. He wants us to understand that if we know Christ the Logos then we know the one who has been from eternity, always is, and ever will be, face to face with the heavenly Father.

As Christians then, we have come to know the one who brought the cosmos into being, without whom nothing – including ourselves

---

[1] See John 10:30-38.

[2] John 14:9.

[3] John 20:28. John's Gospel is structured with a Prologue (John 1:1-18) and an Epilogue (John 21:1-25). The central narrative therefore runs from 1:19 to 20:31. In this context Thomas' confession is the climax to the entire Gospel. It is as though John were saying, 'Everything I said about Jesus in the Prologue, and expanded throughout this Gospel, now comes to fruition in the faith and confession of Thomas! Indeed I have written the Gospel so that others may come to believe who have not seen Jesus. For he himself promised, "Blessed are those who have not seen and yet have believed."'

[4] This is well expressed in B. F. Westcott, *The Gospel According to John* (originally part of *The Speaker's Commentary*, 1881; repr. Grand Rapids, MI: Wm B. Eerdmans, 1951), 3: 'It is necessarily without the article … inasmuch as it describes the nature of the Word and does not identify His Person. It would be pure Sabellianism to say "The Word was ὁ θεός."' Sabellianism (named after Sabellius) was a form of Modalism, *i.e.*, the teaching that the one God variously manifested himself as Father, Son, or Spirit – but they were not distinct Persons, only roles, or modes of being.

– has been brought into being. We know him as the one who 'is at the Father's side'. His incarnation does not diminish his identity. Indeed, as Jesus himself prayed, 'This is eternal life, that they may know you the only true God, and Jesus Christ whom you have sent.'[1]

And so these opening words of John's Gospel teach us emphatically that we must never think it is a small thing to become a Christian. The reverse is the truth: it is the grandest, the greatest, the largest and the most mind-stretching experience of human existence. He who was in the beginning 'face to face' with God has come in order to be 'face to face' with us, so that we may live 'face to face' with him!

Incarnate Son

John goes on to emphasize the Saviour's self-humbling.

If we fast forward to John 1:14 we are now told that this Word who is eternal deity 'became flesh and dwelt among us'. He became part of his own creation.

Here is more food for thought.

The eternal Word of God dwelt in the presence of his heavenly Father, surrounded by angels, archangels, cherubim and seraphim.[2] He lived in an atmosphere of intense purity, in personal communion with his Father and with the Holy Spirit.

In this heavenly world angelic creatures praise him, but so feel the intensity of the purity of God that they veil their faces in awe.[3] Although themselves perfectly holy and without sin, they clearly sense their creatureliness. It is as though their own created holiness is not able fully to bear the infinite intensity of the uncreated holiness of the mutual devotion they sense is expressed among the three persons of the Trinity.

So this for John is the wonder of the incarnation. The one who was able to live 'face to face' with God in that holy atmosphere, and to gaze into the eyes of his Father, has assumed our flesh and come to live 'face to face' with us in our fallen world, in obedience to his Father.

[1] John 17:3.
[2] John notes that when Isaiah had his stunning encounter with the thrice holy Lord, praised by the six-winged heavenly seraphim, the experience at least included a sight of the glory of the Son of God. Compare Isaiah 6:1-10 with John 12:40-41.
[3] Isaiah 6:2.

> Christ, by highest Heav'n adored;
> Christ the everlasting Lord; …
> Veiled in flesh the Godhead see;
> Hail the Incarnate Deity,
> Pleased as Man with men to dwell,
> Jesus our Immanuel.[1]

We have no measure to calculate what that must have meant for him.

'From highest bliss to such a world as this'[2]

Isaiah had a moment of life-changing access to this heavenly world. His encounter with God in his infinite holiness affected all of his senses – sight, hearing, taste, touch, and smell.[3] He saw the Lord; he heard a voice; he felt the foundations of the thresholds of the building shake; the house was filled with smoke; and a burning coal touched the prophet's lips.

The Son of God must have experienced this *in reverse* as it were, when 'the Word became flesh and dwelt among us'.

Pollution and a Parable

Many air travellers today do not remember the days when smoking on aeroplanes was permitted. The 'smoking section' was at the rear of the plane. On a large plane, for example on a transatlantic crossing, the smoking and non-smoking sections were separated by a curtain. If you are allergic to cigarette smoke you can probably imagine the intense discomfort of a long night in economy class crossing the Atlantic! Or take one step further in your imagination. The 'non-smoking' seats are all booked and occupied. You are seated in the middle seat of the five central seats of a jumbo jet. There is no escape.

Even today, when smokers are exiled from buildings to the area just outside, you hold your breath for the first ten yards of your exit. And when a smoker comes into the elevator just as the doors are closing to accompany you on your ascent, every breath he or she takes fills the confined space.

---

[1] From the hymn by Charles Wesley (1707–78), 'Hark! the herald angels sing.'
[2] From the hymn by Edward Caswall (1814–78), 'See! In yonder manger low.'
[3] See Isaiah 6:4, 6-7. Thereafter he sees God as 'the Holy One'.

The irritating paradox, of course, is that only the non-smokers notice. To the smokers – they themselves, their clothes, their breath – all smell quite normal.

Think of this as a metaphor for our fallen world where sin impregnates the atmosphere and is our native air.

Or imagine this scenario:

The owner of an apartment building lives in the penthouse suite with its balcony and magnificent garden. The atmosphere is 'heavenly', unpolluted by smokers.

But now the owner enters the elevator. He descends to the ground floor. The doors open. The lobby is full of smokers. The atmosphere is alien and indeed noxious. He cannot avoid breathing it in. Worse, the smokers breathe all over him. Then they see he is not smoking, and insist he does. They offer him their expensive cigarette cases, but the very smell of the unsmoked contents is repulsive to him. They become angry and insist he smoke, and despise him for not joining them. They deliberately inhale and then push their faces in front of his, exhaling in his eyes, nose, and mouth. They press their burning cigarettes on him. There is no escape for the owner.

Can you imagine that? The only word to describe it would seem to be – significantly – excruciating.

Yet this is but a parable.

There is something almost distasteful about thinking of the perfectly holy (not merely *sin-less*) One coming 'in the likeness of sinful flesh' (literally, 'the likeness of the flesh of sin').[1] When the Word became flesh this world must have been almost unbearable for him.

So John is saying: 'Grasp the magnitude of the difference between being the eternal Holy Son in the presence of the Father and the Spirit and living in a depraved world breathing the atmosphere created by sinful men and women.' Wonder of wonders, 'the Word became flesh' – or perhaps we might express it, 'the Word was born in flesh'.

This does not mean that the eternal Word was transformed, or minimized his deity in any sense. Rather he remained the eternal Word as he came into the world in flesh and blood. He really became one of us, flesh of our flesh, and bone of our bone.[2] As the Fathers

[1] Romans 8:3.
[2] A point emphasized in Hebrews 2:14.

of the Christian church rightly saw, he is eternally one divine person with a divine nature, but was conceived in the womb of the Virgin Mary, sharing our human nature. He lived his life in terms of both of these natures.

Why was this so important? Because only a divine person could do anything to save us. None of us is capable of saving either ourselves or anyone else. On the other hand only someone with a *human* nature is qualified to be a substitute and sacrifice for human sinners.[1] As again the Church Fathers delighted to put it, the Son of God became what he was not in order that we might become what we were not.

Truly God, truly man; fully God, fully man

'Incarnation' means that Jesus was truly and fully God and truly and fully man. His humanity did not experience an injection of deity in order to boost him for his work. Rather he came to live among us as the Word become flesh. He came as one person who functioned appropriately according to each of his two natures. According to his divine nature he functioned as the creating and sustaining Word. The babe in the manger continued to uphold his own universe. And yet, according to his human nature, he was tired and thirsty, calm and joyful, sad and hungry, amazed, sorrowful and, ultimately, crucified.

This is difficult to understand. But that is so *by definition*. There is no analogy to which we can point to say 'It is like that.' The incarnation is a singularity. So we must resist any tendency to reduce Christ to manageable proportions. In fact, right from his first words John the Gospel writer is saying, 'Do not be reductionist! No! Grasp hold of the magnitude of the reality.'

Neither John nor any of the other writers of the Scriptures pauses to explain this to us. How could they? For this is what Paul called 'the mystery of godliness: He was manifested in the flesh.'[2] But at the same time this mystery is the key to understanding the Gospels. Not only so, it is the key to life. We can no more penetrate it than we can stare at the full glory of the sun. But like the sun this Son shines his light into our lives with the result that everything else becomes clearer.

[1] Hebrews 2:17.
[2] 1 Timothy 3:16.

At first glance we might think that John's teaching is completely different from the other Gospel writers. John's Prologue gives no role to either Mary or Joseph, whereas Matthew and Luke, at least on the surface, seem to involve them in his coming.

Does this mean that Matthew and Luke held a different view of the incarnation from that of John? No. But they did look at the same event from different perspectives. For it is just as clear in Matthew and Luke that Joseph was set aside when it came to the conception of Jesus. However much we admire his response to the announcement of Jesus' coming, Joseph played no active part in it. Indeed, while Mary yielded to the word of the Lord, the conception of Jesus in her womb was not something in which she consciously participated. All that took place she experienced mysteriously, unconsciously (although she knew it would happen), and completely passively.

So from this point of view the message is the same in Luke and Matthew as it is in John's Gospel. What, then, does John emphasize? This: in the incarnation of the Word, *God himself was sovereignly at work to bring salvation.*

Yet if Jesus' conception was supernatural, his birth was normal. John of Damascus, the great theologian of the Eastern Church, had a beautiful way of describing this: 'The conception, indeed, was through the sense of hearing, but the birth through the usual path by which children come.'[1] Mary was altogether passive in the conception, and yet at the same time she was active in her submission to the will of the Lord and, clearly, in the process of his birth.[2] The whole nine-month-long event was thus a further illustration of a biblical pattern in which God accomplishes his most powerful works in darkness: at first creation, at the cross of Calvary, in the garden tomb in the resurrection, and here in the coming of his Son, in the darkness of the womb

---

[1] John of Damascus (A.D. 675–749), *Exposition of the Orthodox Faith, Nicene and Post Nicene Fathers*, second series, ed. P. Schaff and H. Weir, tr. S. D. F. Salmond (repr. Peabody MS: Hendricksen Publishers, 2004), vol. 9, *Hilary of Poitiers and John of Damascus.* The quotation is from p. 86 of the section on John of Damascus.

[2] Mary was of course 'active' in the birth of Jesus. For it was his conception, not his birth, that was supernatural. His birth was completely natural – Mary too must have felt the fulfilment of God's word in Genesis 3:16: 'In pain you shall bring forth children.'

of the Virgin. Thus silently, privately, humbly, hidden from proud or prying human eyes, the Son of God came in our flesh.

Real and holy flesh

'The child to be born will be called holy', the angel Gabriel told Mary.[1] The New Testament expresses the significance of this in a variety of ways. These safeguard us from a fairly common assumption Christians make, namely that Jesus' combination of divinity and perfect sanctity made life somehow easier for him.

The truth is in many respects the very reverse. Swimming against the tide is never easier. Being spiritually sensitive makes this sinful world a much more painful place in which to live. A man who is devoted to his wife finds it more, not less difficult to be at ease in a working environment where other men speak of women as objects to be conquered, or used for selfish pleasure.

This carries important implications.

We have never truly and fully tasted or sensed how sinful sin is because it is so normal to us. Jesus, by contrast, saw how abnormal, distorting, ugly, and deeply rebellious it really is. Nor have we tasted weakness or need to the extent the strong and rich Son of God did. Nor have we felt as sorrowful as the Lord Jesus, nor experienced shame the way he did – all in his perfectly holy humanity. Where we have become insensitive he was perfectly, purely, wholly sensitive.

We all know people who are sensitive. Some people are musically sensitive. While we listen to a symphony we may be thinking 'this is a great performance', but the sensitive musician is jarred by every wrong note, every misplayed chord, every misinterpretation of the conductor. Other people are more sensitive in different ways, to sights, to sounds, even to smells. And some are more sensitive to other people. They have an instinct that senses when someone else is disappointed or sore, or pretending, or depressed. Others have no sensitivity like that.

But can you imagine being fully sensitive to human sickness, and sorrow, and sin? That is what John means when he says that 'the Word became flesh'.

---

[1] Luke 1:35.

Salvation

Thus far we have noticed John's stress on the divine origin of the Word, and his self-humbling. There is one further emphasis we find in his Prologue: the Word of God assumed our flesh in order that he might bear our sins and bring us salvation.

As John expands on his understanding of the incarnation, he explains why it is that the Son of God came.

'He came', writes John, 'as the light to give illumination to darkened minds.'[1] Later he tells us that by nature we love the darkness rather than the light, because only there can we hide from God and feel secure in our sin.[2] And then we begin to get used to the darkness, perhaps even eventually claiming that the darkness is normal – that it is our 'light'. Alas, said Jesus, for if the light that is in us is actually darkness then how great is that darkness![3]

If my heart and mind were full of light I would love God with all my heart and mind. But by nature I love him with neither. I may naïvely say that 'God is love' when what I really mean is that he is tolerant of the fact that I do not love him. How darkened is my mind? Is it so darkened by nature that I think that Jesus Christ is not really worthy of everything I have to give?

But the narrative line of John's Gospel tells us how Jesus brought light into the darkness. He shone light into the mental darkness in the mind of Nicodemus, and into the moral darkness of the woman he met at the well at Sychar, and into the darkness death brought into the Bethany home of Mary and Martha when their brother Lazarus died.[4]

That is our need exactly. We need to see him as he really is and not as we imagine he was. Not as a 'great moral teacher', or as a convenience to help us along in life, but as the inextinguishable Light who shines in the darkness.[5]

John then goes on to say that from this same Christ we receive 'grace upon grace' (John 1:16).

Why do we need so much grace? For our sins.

[1] John 1:9.
[2] John 3:19.
[3] Matthew 6:23.
[4] See John 3, 4, and 11 for the narratives.
[5] John 1:4-5.

We need forgiveness and justification. The Word was made flesh in order to provide them.

More than that we are also spiritually dead in our trespasses and sins.[1] The Word is the life-giver who gives us new birth and new life by the power of his Spirit.

We are also alienated from God. But the Word has come to bring us adoption into his family: 'to all who did receive him, who believed in his name, he gave the right to become the children of God'.[2]

For John, as for Paul, our tragedy is that we were created as the image of God to reflect his character, but now 'fall short of the glory of God'.[3] Alas, that glory was marred in Adam and inevitably also in us.

But now John tells us that in Jesus Christ the recovery of our destiny has begun. In the Word made flesh we once again see the glory of God. By the end of the Gospel we will be able to hear Jesus pray, not only for John and his fellow apostles, but also for all of us who believe in Christ through their word:

> The glory that you have given me I have given to them ...
> Father, I desire that they also, whom you have given me, may
> be with me where I am, to see my glory ...[4]

Is it really so surprising then that angels burst out of heaven when the news broke that the Word had become flesh and was living among men?

> Who is He in yonder stall,
> At whose feet the shepherds fall?
>
> *'Tis the Lord, the King of glory.*
> *'Tis the Lord, O wondrous story.*
> *At his feet we humbly fall.*
> *Crown Him, crown Him Lord of all.*[5]

Faith in Christ rising within us is, surely, the only fitting response.

[1] Ephesians 2:5.

[2] John 1:12.

[3] See Paul's comments in Romans 3:23. 'We have all sinned' he notes. This involves breaking God's commandments, of course. But here the apostle paints sin on the larger canvas of the glory of God – that is the expression of all that God is in all of his divine person and attributes.

[4] John 17:22, 24.

[5] From the hymn 'Who is He in yonder stall' by Benjamin Russell Hanby (1833–67).

But do you have faith? Have you sensed your real need? Have you received Christ? Have you tasted the sense of relief, the joy, and the peace of God which comes by trusting in him and receiving him? Then of course you will want to know and love him. And of course you will

Crown Him Lord of all.

So be sure you have taken the monumental step that changes absolutely everything. And then you will never slip back into thinking that becoming a Christian is simply one of life's added extras. No! It is life itself given to us by the Word incarnate who said, 'I am come that they may have life and have it abundantly.'[1]

Thank God that the Word who was with God, and who is God, was also made flesh! And thank God if indeed you have seen his glory!

[1] John 10:10.

2. The River – *Baptism*

Who is He in Jordan's River
Takes our place as tho' a sinner?
  'Tis the Lord! O wondrous story!
  'Tis the Lord! the King of glory!
  At His feet we humbly fall;
  Crown Him, Crown Him Lord of all.

Matthew 3:1-17

In those days John the Baptist came preaching in the wilderness of Judea, ² 'Repent, for the kingdom of heaven is at hand.' ³ For this is he who was spoken of by the prophet Isaiah when he said,

'The voice of one crying in the wilderness:
"Prepare the way of the Lord;
make his paths straight."'

⁴ Now John wore a garment of camel's hair and a leather belt around his waist, and his food was locusts and wild honey. ⁵ Then Jerusalem and all Judea and all the region about the Jordan were going out to him, ⁶ and they were baptized by him in the river Jordan, confessing their sins.

⁷ But when he saw many of the Pharisees and Sadducees coming for baptism, he said to them, 'You brood of vipers! Who warned you to flee from the wrath to come? ⁸ Bear fruit in keeping with repentance. ⁹ And do not presume to say to yourselves, "We have Abraham as our father," for I tell you, God is able from these stones to raise up children for Abraham. ¹⁰ Even now the axe is laid to the root of the trees. Every tree therefore that does not bear good fruit is cut down and thrown into the fire.

¹¹ 'I baptize you with water for repentance, but he who is coming after me is mightier than I, whose sandals I am not worthy to carry. He will baptize you with the Holy Spirit and with fire. ¹² His winnowing fork is in his hand, and he will clear his threshing floor and gather his wheat into the barn, but the chaff he will burn with unquenchable fire.'

¹³ Then Jesus came from Galilee to the Jordan to John, to be baptized by him. ¹⁴ John would have prevented him, saying, 'I need to be baptized by you, and do you come to me?' ¹⁵ But Jesus answered him, 'Let it be so now, for thus it is fitting for us to fulfil all righteousness.' Then he consented. ¹⁶ And when Jesus was baptized, immediately he went up from the water, and behold, the heavens were opened to him, and he saw the Spirit of God descending like a dove and coming to rest on him; ¹⁷ and behold, a voice from heaven said, 'This is my beloved Son, with whom I am well pleased.'

WE turn now to the second 'major' event in the life of Jesus. It took place some thirty years after his birth. His baptism in the River Jordan was an event of such significance that it is recorded in all four Gospels.

Here we will follow Matthew's account.

But first we need to set this significant event in its context.

Baptisms at the River Jordan

John the Baptist appears very suddenly in the gospel story. Since the opening narratives in Luke's Gospel we have heard nothing about him. Now, three decades on he emerges as a preacher. His burden was to call people to repent – to turn from their sin.

John was the first prophet to appear in Jerusalem or in its environs for four centuries. His ministry brought to a close what had seemed an endless period of divine silence. Like an unexpected storm cloud he came over the horizon, with his strange garb and ascetic diet. His appearance must have seemed well married to the searing words he spoke about sin and judgment.

According to Matthew people came to hear him in vast numbers:

> Jerusalem and all Judea and all the region about the Jordan
> were going out to him, and they were baptized by him in
> the River Jordan, confessing their sins.[1]

So they came, perhaps in their tens of thousands, or even, as some have suggested, in hundreds of thousands. A massive spiritual awakening seemed to be underway.

John's baptism was not Christian baptism. For one thing it was not baptism in the name of the Trinity. Nor was its focus on redemption and deliverance, resurrection and new life. Rather it was a baptism of

---

[1] Matthew 3:5-6.

confession of sin and repentance. But where did this baptism come from? Where did John get the idea?

There already was a baptismal ceremony for Gentiles who became adherents of Judaism, uniting themselves to the Lord and his covenant. They were unclean by definition, and therefore unfit for the presence of God or for table fellowship with Jews. They needed to be washed. So they were baptized as a symbol of the washing away of their sins. John's baptism spoke of uncleanness in precisely the same way these Gentile proselyte baptisms did.

There were, of course, various cleansing rituals, or washings, in the Old Testament. Hebrews 9:10 mentions these. In English versions the word 'washings' is used, but in fact the Greek word is *baptisms*. In addition there were various cleansing rituals common among some of the Jewish sects like the Essenes and the Qumran community.[1] Baptisms of various kinds were therefore well known rituals.

John's baptism however carried a significance all of its own.

For one thing he chose to baptize at the River Jordan.

This was the very place where Israel had crossed over into the Promised Land, after being led through the wilderness for forty years following the Exodus.[2]

Here, too, Elijah had been last seen at the close of his ministry before being taken to heaven.[3]

Thus, John, whom Jesus identified as the Elijah who was expected to return before the Day of the Lord,[4] had both the appearance and the message of the divinely appointed herald of the end of the age. Now was the hour for radical repentance, and baptism was its symbol.

What happened next, however, is surprising, even shocking.

Jesus came to John and asked to be baptized.

If we are to make sense of this we need to notice several features of this dramatic event.

---

[1] The people associated with what we call 'The Dead Sea Scrolls' which were discovered in 1947 in caves near the north-western end of the Dead Sea.

[2] See Joshua 3:1-17.

[3] 2 Kings 2:6-14.

[4] Malachi 4:5-6. See Matthew 11:13-14.

Baptism

First of all we are given a description of the baptism of Jesus. We may be so familiar with it that we know what is coming and we remain relatively unmoved by it. But it was wholly unexpected – not least to John, who was of course a relative of Jesus.[1]

Here is John, steeped in the prophecies of the Old Testament and in the expectation of God's Messiah. He sees himself fulfilling ancient prophecy, as the 'voice crying in the wilderness: "Prepare the way of the Lord."'[2]

He clearly knew he had a vital role to play in the fulfilment of Old Testament prophecy. But now Jesus comes from Galilee to the Jordan River, perhaps at the end of a long day of baptisms, when the crowds have dissipated a little. He asks to be baptized. John argues with him, and 'would have prevented him'.[3] He realized who Jesus really was – the Messiah. He had no need of any baptism, certainly not of this baptism of repentance. Resistance was therefore John's first reaction.

What was John thinking? When he first sensed God's call to baptize, was he (as Paul and Peter would later be) reminded of certain events in the Old Testament connected with water? Paul talks about baptism 'into Moses … in the sea'. He is thinking about how the people of the Exodus passed through the Red Sea on dry ground while the Egyptians were destroyed. The same event was an act of salvation for God's people while it was an act of judgment on the Egyptians.[4]

Peter saw the Flood and the deliverance of Noah and his three sons and their wives in the ark as an analogy of baptism: it was a deluge, a water ordeal, a kind of baptism.[5]

Judgment

These baptisms – the Flood and the drowning of the Egyptians in the Red Sea – were water ordeals of terrible and catastrophic judgment. They were indicative of the wrath of God, of what happens to the

---

[1] Elizabeth, John's mother is said to be a 'relative' of Mary the mother of Jesus, Luke 1:36.

[2] Matthew 3:3; the quotation is from Isaiah 40:3.

[3] Matthew 3:14.

[4] 1 Corinthians 10:1-2. The event itself is described in Exodus 14:1-31.

[5] 1 Peter 3:18-22.

faithless individual or the community that is not redeemed and whose sins are not forgiven. Yet through these baptisms those who had faith in God's provision found refuge and were saved from his wrath.

If this was any part of John's thinking about baptism, no wonder his reaction to Jesus was: 'I need to be baptized by you. If anyone deserves the baptism of judgment, it is I not you.' But Jesus responded: 'Let it be so now, for thus it is fitting for us to fulfil all righteousness.'[1]

What did he mean?

Jesus' statement probably echoes some words from Isaiah 53, the fourth and most familiar of a series of 'songs' in the second half of Isaiah's prophetic book. These songs describe and interpret the life and suffering of a figure simply described as 'my Servant'.[2] We read of a fulfilling of righteousness through his life:

> By his knowledge shall the righteous one, my servant,
>> make many to be accounted righteous,
>> and he shall bear their iniquities.[3]

Jesus had come to be that Servant, to identify himself with us in our sin, and to become the one who would bear the iniquities of his people.

John's baptism then was a kind of declaration of war against the sins of God's people because they had violated his covenant. He had made the covenant with them in his grace and love, but they had persistently failed to be faithful to its obligations. So now there is an ultimatum. John's baptism is a clarion call for repentance. John stands as the prosecuting counsel; he now presents a divine lawsuit against his contemporaries. For God is declaring a judgment against them as catastrophic as the Flood in the time of Noah or as the drowning of the Egyptians in the time of Moses.

It is *this* baptism Jesus insists on receiving.

---

[1] Matthew 3:15.
[2] The songs are in chapters 42, 49, 50 and 52-53.
[3] Isaiah 53:11.

The name of a sinner

Baptism is also a naming ritual. In Christian baptism we are 'named' for the Trinity.[1] In a similar way, Jesus is being 'named' here in his Jordan River baptism.

Forget for the moment the controversial issues related to baptism – the how and the when and the how much – and focus on the *meaning* of what is happening. It is the supremely important issue here. For in this baptism of judgment, John is declaring to Jesus, 'You are here named among sinners; you are someone who is identified with covenant-breakers.' In this sense, Jesus is being 'named [numbered] with the transgressors'.[2] From now on, we might say, his name is 'Sinner'. John Calvin puts it boldly:

> He willed in full measure to appear before the judgment seat of God his Father in the name and in the person of all sinners, being then ready to be condemned, inasmuch as he bore our burden.[3]

This is the new identity taken by the holy and impeccable one who, from the time of his birth, had grown in wisdom and stature and in favour with God and man.[4] Jesus is thirty years old now,[5] the age when priests entered into their full ministry. He has never sinned, never broken any of God's commandments. He has never left undone those things that he ought to have done, or done those things which he ought not to have done. No wicked thought had ever seeped into his consciousness. He had never yielded to any temptation. He was holy, innocent, unstained, and separated from sinners.[6] No wonder John had said, 'I need to be baptized by you.'

But Jesus' response is this:

> Trust me, John. Baptize me so that we might fulfil the calling our Father in heaven has given to us both. I am indeed the Messiah. I identify now with your baptism of judgment in

[1] Matthew 28:19.

[2] Isaiah 53:12.

[3] John Calvin, *Sermons on the Deity of Christ*, selected and translated by Leroy Nixon (Grand Rapids: Wm B. Eerdmans, 1950), 52.

[4] Luke 2:52.

[5] Luke 3:23.

[6] Hebrews 7:26.

this baptism of repentance. But this water baptism only points to a final ordeal to which I will one day submit. My coming baptism will not be symbolic, but real. For then I will be baptized not with water but with my own blood.

This, then, is the inner significance of Jesus' baptism. It is as though he is being named a covenant-violator. He is identifying himself with us in our sins. Symbolically the water into which the sins of the repentant people have been washed is now pouring over his head! He is taking them upon himself as our Sin-Bearer and Saviour.

Our Lord's baptism is therefore an act of *substitution*. Jesus is undergoing what we deserve to undergo. He takes our place because

> There was no other good enough
> To pay the price of sin.
> He only could unlock the gate
> Of heaven, and let us in.[1]

And so John yields, and baptizes him with the water of judgment. Jesus embraces the curse. When Paul says that the people of God were baptized into Moses and into the Sea, not a drop of water touched them. The Egyptians received the curse; but God's people got the blessing. So it will be when our Lord's symbolic baptism becomes a reality. The curse he bears is ours; the blessing we receive is his.

Here at the Jordan we see the reason why the great exchange at the heart of the gospel is possible. Why are we forgiven? Why do we go free? Why are we blessed? Why do we get the promise of entering the Promised Land? Because Jesus takes the curse. That is what his baptism means.

Later James and John came to Jesus and asked for the chief places in Jesus' kingdom. (We want to hide our faces in embarrassment that they should make such a request, except that we are no better!) Do you remember how Jesus responded? 'Are you able … to be baptized with the baptism with which I am baptized?'[2] He was talking about his baptism at Calvary. The reality to which the waters of Jordan pointed, polluted as they were with the sins of the people, was the flood waters

---

[1] From the hymn by Cecil Frances Alexander (1818–95), 'There is a green hill far away.'

[2] Mark 10:38.

of the *anathema* of God against sinners. That is what his baptism meant! He took the curse that is the just reward of a covenant-violator in order that we might receive the divine blessing as though we were covenant-keepers.

It is into this pattern of baptism that our baptism fits. Just as his water baptism in Jordan pointed forwards to his real baptism on Calvary, so ours points back to it. Thus when we are baptized into union with Christ it is into *his death* which draws both the guilt and sting of sin, and into *his resurrection* through which we are raised into a new life altogether.[1] And it all begins at the River Jordan.

Once we have grasped this we are in a position to examine further elements in this event.

Anointing

As Jesus stepped out of the River Jordan – perhaps as he stood on the river bank – 'the heavens were opened'. Mark's briefer account uses a more violent term: the heavens were 'torn open'.[2] The words seem to echo the prayer of Isaiah 64:1: 'Oh that you would rend the heavens and come down.' Now the Day of the Lord was dawning, the Messiah had come, and the heavens were opening.

Something cataclysmic is happening here; 'earth shattering' in the fullest sense of what that ultimately entails. For Christ came to inaugurate a new creation. He came to repair what was marred by Adam: the old is going to be made new. A new creation, a new heavens and a new earth will be brought about as a result of the baptism of Jesus. So the heavens open in anticipation of what still awaits its consummation in the future.

But in addition the Spirit of God descended on Jesus in the form of a dove.

What a beautiful image! Have you ever seen slow-motion pictures of a dove landing in all its sheer gracefulness? You could scarcely imagine, and certainly not create, anything more beautiful than that.

The imagery immediately brings to mind a significant moment in the Old Testament. Indeed more than one.

[1] Romans 6:1-4; Colossians 2:12.
[2] Matthew 3:16; Mark 1:10.

We have already alluded to Noah, the Flood, and the ark which Simon Peter saw as a picture of baptism. When the rains had stopped and the waters receded, Noah sent out from the ark a dove that later returned with an olive leaf in its mouth. It was the sign that the judgment of God had passed and that a 'new creation' had begun.

In addition, there is here, surely, also an echo of the first chapter of Genesis. At the very beginning of creation, when 'the earth was without form and void', the Spirit of God was 'hovering above the waters'.[1] The Hebrew verb word translated 'hover' is *rachaph*. It could also be translated 'fluttering' – like the fluttering of the wings of a bird.[2] So perhaps there is also an allusion here to the original creation. Now, through Jesus' identification with covenant-breakers, God is going to bring about not only the redemption and regeneration of individuals but something far grander even than that – a new creation altogether.

So at the River Jordan the Spirit descended on Jesus now as a sign of the magnitude of the role into which he was publicly entering.

But what does the Spirit's coming say *to Jesus*?

He has come to help him, indwell him, minister to him, strengthen him, empower him, endow him with gifts, and – as what followed his baptism made clear – to lead him into spiritual warfare and victory.

It is worth emphasizing here again that Jesus does not resort to his divine nature in order to accomplish what needs to be done in our human nature. No. Were he to do that, he would no longer be the second man, the last Adam. He would no longer be our representative. We could not say of him that he 'in every respect has been tempted *as we are*, yet without sin'.[3]

What then accounts for Jesus' faithfulness to God? The answer is that from the beginning to the end of his life he was empowered and strengthened in his human nature by the Holy Spirit. He was incarnate by the Holy Spirit. He was conceived by the power of the Holy Spirit in the womb of the Virgin Mary. He grew by the Spirit.

---

[1] Genesis 1:2.

[2] 'Here it describes the action of an eagle hovering over its young before it flies off.' Gordon J. Wenham, *Genesis 1–15* (Waco, TX: Word Books, 1987), 17. The only other occurrence of the verb is in Deuteronomy 32:11.

[3] Hebrews 4:15.

But now he is entering a new phase of his life and ministry. Now comes the prolonged war for which he had been in preparation these past thirty years. Now the Spirit comes to equip him for this new stage of his Messianic work. Now, as we will see in the next chapter, the Spirit will drive him into the wilderness to encounter the great enemy, Satan. And until the end, even in his death, as the author of Hebrews suggests, he will be upheld by the Spirit.[1]

However, before we move on, we should pause to look again at the picture his baptism sets before us.

Who is present here? Do you see the presence of the Trinity?

Jesus, the *Son*, is here, consecrating himself to fulfil his Messianic ministry. The *Spirit* has descended on him to sustain him in his saving work. And now we are about to hear the voice of the *Father*.

Confirmation

The next element in Jesus' baptism is an audible voice from heaven. This is not the last time the heavenly voice is heard.[2] On this occasion it speaks in order to identify Jesus as God's Son and to inaugurate him into his public Messianic ministry.

Later, when the disciple band was seeking a replacement for Judas, Peter said that it was essential to choose someone who had been with Jesus, 'beginning from the baptism of John until the day when he was taken up from us'.[3] Clearly, then, Jesus' baptism was seen by himself and, at least in retrospect, by the apostles, as the first stage of his role as a public representative of sinners.

Several important Old Testament echoes can be heard in the words of the heavenly voice.

The Father speaks and says 'This is my Son, my [or the] Beloved, with whom I am well pleased.'[4]

There is an echo here of the very first of the Servant Songs in Isaiah: 'Behold my servant, whom I uphold, my chosen, in whom my soul delights.'[5]

[1] Hebrews 9:14.
[2] See Matthew 17:5; John 12:27-8.
[3] Acts 1:22.
[4] Matthew 3:17, ESV fn. 1.
[5] Isaiah 42:1.

Jesus must have spent his entire life-time, from his earliest days as a little child at home and in the synagogue in Nazareth, learning, memorizing, and meditating on the Old Testament. The 'Servant Songs' in Isaiah 42, 49, 50, and 52-53 became woven into the very fabric of his being. They spoke of him and of his mission and ministry. The first of them is echoed here, as though the Father is saying, 'I am well pleased with you. Do you remember? Do you remember what Isaiah said?'

There is also perhaps an echo of Genesis 22:2, in which Abraham is challenged to see if he is willing to part with Isaac, the son he loved: 'This is my *beloved son*.'[1]

And in addition, there seems to be a clear echo here of Psalm 2:7 – a hugely significant psalm for the apostles' understanding of the kingdom of Christ:[2] 'You are my son.' The whole psalm speaks of a king before whom the rebellious nations of the world will one day bow.

Some students of Scripture think that these words may also have been meant to confirm to the *human* mind of Jesus his identity as the second person of the Trinity. He must be assured of that identity if he is to fulfil his ministry. Everything around him will speak to the contrary. For how can this *man* be himself *God*? So, as Jesus takes this critical step forward into a journey that inexorably leads to Calvary, the Father opens heaven itself to reassure him:

> My Son, you are my Son! I love you. I want you to know that, and to be absolutely assured of it as you go on this journey that will lead to the abyss of Calvary. I want you to know I have loved you; I do love you; I will always love you.

The hour would come, some three years later, when the Father's face would be shrouded in deep darkness. It would be all that the Son could do to remember that these words had been spoken from heaven at his baptism. Then Jesus would not cry out, 'My Father, my Father, you love me!' but, 'My God, my God, why have you forsaken me?'[3] Did he lose all consciousness of his sonship? All the more reason for the Father who loved him to say now:

[1] See Genesis 22:1.
[2] See, for example, Acts 4:23-31.
[3] Matthew 27:46.

I want you to know this now, my Son. It will still be true when you cannot feel it or see it: I love you. I am well pleased with you. It will be important *then* to remember the voice that speaks *now.*

Active obedience

In summary, then, Jesus' baptism is an act of obedience. In submission to the Father's plan he is publicly identified as the covenant-breaker who is taking the the place of Adam and his posterity. He becomes the sin-bearer before the judgment seat of God.

On 1 January 1937, Dr J. Gresham Machen, the founder of Westminster Theological Seminary in Philadelphia, sent a brief but deeply-moving telegram to his colleague Professor John Murray. Machen was the most significant and scholarly of the figures who took part in the controversy with liberal theology in the era that followed the First World War. At great personal cost he, with others, left Princeton Seminary to form Westminster Seminary in 1929. Over the Christmas break at the end of 1936 he had gone to help some of the small churches in North Dakota, but took ill and was hospitalized with pneumonia. In the previous few weeks he had been engaged in deep discussion with John Murray about what theologians have called 'the active obedience of Christ' – namely that Christ not only *suffered for us,* but actively *obeyed for us* throughout the whole course of his life ('becoming obedient to the point of death, even death on a cross'[1]). Thus our justification includes not only the pardon of our sins but the counting of Christ's righteousness to us.

Machen had apparently struggled with this teaching, but in his sickness he came to grasp its significance. On his deathbed, between bouts of unconsciousness, he dictated a telegram to Murray: 'I'm so thankful for active obedience of Christ. No hope without it.'[2] Later that day the fifty-five year old Machen died.

This is what we see in Jesus: an active obedience. He is obedient to his Father for us.

[1] Philippians 2:8.
[2] Ned B. Stonehouse, *J. Gresham Machen, A Biographical Memoir* (Grand Rapids, MI: Wm B. Eerdmans, 1955), 508.

As the Father looked on the one to whom he spoke, as the Spirit came upon the one who had been baptized, as, doubtless, the angels looked down in wonder at their king, Jesus now stepped out of the water of the River Jordan publicly identified as Saviour, irreversibly committed to fulfil his Father's wishes as the sin-bearer we so desperately need.

Earlier John the Baptist had spoken to the Pharisees and Sadducees who had come to investigate (and probably to critique and condemn) what he was doing. He had a word of warning for them: 'Do not presume to say to yourselves, "We have Abraham as our Father."'[1] Having Abraham as their Father would count for nothing on the Day of Judgment. In fact it would count against them. Indeed all the privileges they had enjoyed would at the last count against them. What they needed was somebody to stand in their place, to bear their guilt. They needed a substitute. They needed a Saviour.

That is what we all need: to have a substitute, to have a Saviour – this is our only hope on the Day of Judgment. What will be of vital importance to us then is to know that Christ accepted our curse in the River Jordan, and then bore its implications on the cross of Calvary so that we might receive the blessings of which our baptism speaks. Thus through faith we receive the forgiveness of sin; the cleansing of heart and conscience; the blessings of being reckoned a covenant-keeper; receiving an inheritance with Christ, and having the hope of the resurrection to everlasting life and glory.

In a word, since Christ has fulfilled all that was symbolized at the River Jordan, we now hear the voice of the Father saying to us in the gospel, 'Now that you believe in my Son, the Lord Jesus Christ, as Saviour and Lord, you are my sons. Be assured that I love you.'

[1] Matthew 3:9.

3. The Wilderness – *Temptation*

Who is He, in deep distress
Fasting in the wilderness?

'Tis the Lord! O wondrous story!
'Tis the Lord! the King of glory!
At His feet we humbly fall;
Crown Him, Crown Him Lord of all.

Luke 4:1-15

And Jesus, full of the Holy Spirit, returned from the Jordan and was led by the Spirit in the wilderness [2] for forty days, being tempted by the devil. And he ate nothing during those days. And when they were ended, he was hungry. [3] The devil said to him, 'If you are the Son of God, command this stone to become bread.' [4] And Jesus answered him, 'It is written, "Man shall not live by bread alone."' [5] And the devil took him up and showed him all the kingdoms of the world in a moment of time, [6] and said to him, 'To you I will give all this authority and their glory, for it has been delivered to me, and I give it to whom I will. [7] If you, then, will worship me, it will all be yours.' [8] And Jesus answered him, 'It is written,

> "You shall worship the Lord your God,
>   and him only shall you serve."'

[9] And he took him to Jerusalem and set him on the pinnacle of the temple and said to him, 'If you are the Son of God, throw yourself down from here, [10] for it is written,

> "He will command his angels concerning you,
>   to guard you,"

[11] and

> "On their hands they will bear you up,
>   lest you strike your foot against a stone."'

[12] And Jesus answered him, 'It is said, "You shall not put the Lord your God to the test."' [13] And when the devil had ended every temptation, he departed from him until an opportune time.

[14] And Jesus returned in the power of the Spirit to Galilee, and a report about him went out through all the surrounding country. [15] And he taught in their synagogues, being glorified by all.

MOST people are familiar with an optical illusion which appears to some to be a beautiful young woman but to others as an old and ugly one. You may know someone (or even be someone!) who has said, 'I've looked but I never see anything except an ugly hag', while others say, 'All I see is a beautiful young woman.'

Yet if you fix your gaze on one particular point in that optical illusion, almost at will you can 'flip' what you see from the ugly old hag to the beautiful young woman, or *vice versa*. But you need to know what to look for!

Something similar is true of the Gospels' accounts of the temptations of Jesus. We get so used to looking at it from one fixed perspective that we tend to miss something that is central in the whole picture.

It is very popular to interpret the account of Jesus' temptations as though it had been written specifically, even exclusively, to teach Christians how to resist their temptations. Probably in many home, neighbourhood, or church Bible study groups these verses are read and the leader's question is, 'What does this passage teach us about how we can resist temptation?'

Now, we do have much we can learn from Jesus about resisting temptation. But that is not the point of this passage. If this is all we see, then the temptation narrative has become an optical illusion to us. For it is not recorded in sacred Scripture to teach *us* how to resist the temptations we experience in common, but to show us *how the Lord Jesus resisted temptations that were unique to him.*

So, if we are suffering from this optical illusion, we need to focus on the point that will change it.

In doing so we may be delivered from a general optical illusion that is commonplace in reading and studying the Gospels, namely looking primarily for what they say to us about our lives, rather than for what they teach us about the life of Jesus.

So what we must do is to leave aside the application of the passage to ourselves and focus on the teaching of the passage about Jesus.

Confronting the enemy

When we shift our focus to Jesus, the first thing we notice is that he was led into the wilderness to confront temptation[1] – whereas temptation comes to us to confront us.

Jesus' temptations are specific and unique to him.

The devil will never tempt you to turn stones into bread, or offer you the kingdoms of this world, or take you to the pinnacle of the Jerusalem temple and urge you to jump down as an expression of your faith. Yes, he has variations on these themes when he comes to us, but there are specific reasons why these were the ways in which he tempted Jesus. So we need to fix our eyes upon Jesus, and say to the passage, 'Tell me, what have you to say about the Saviour?'

Luke's narrative is designed to help us to see Jesus from a very specific perspective. He sets it in a frame that is subtly different from (but not in contradiction of) the accounts of the temptations in Matthew and Mark.

The immediate context in Luke is Jesus' genealogy.[2] It is in a different position from its appearance in Matthew's Gospel. And it contains different elements.[3]

Whereas Matthew begins with Abraham and works forwards to Jesus, Luke begins with Jesus and works backwards not only to Abraham but beyond him to Adam.

Why does he trace the Saviour's bloodline back to Adam? It cannot have been an accident, or done thoughtlessly – not when Luke was such a careful author. He was saying something significant. But what?

The Second Man

Luke was at times a travelling companion of the Apostle Paul. Perhaps this explains why what he seems to be doing here is to express biographically the significance of Jesus' temptations that Paul expressed doctrinally.

[1] Mark, in his brief but significant account of the temptations, uses an even stronger verb: 'The Spirit immediately *drove him out* into the wilderness' (Mark 1:12).

[2] Luke 3:23-38.

[3] See Matthew 1:1-17.

Paul's perspective on history can be described in very basic ways. He understood that God created Adam as the head of creation. He was called to rule over it, to be its king and its cultivator. But he sinned, and dragged the whole race with him while the created order was thrown into reverse gear around him. What flows from Adam is disobedience, judgment, and death. But now God has sent a Second Man, a Last Adam[1] to pay the penalty for Adam's sin, and to throw into forward gear his people's lives and indeed the created order.[2]

This is why we need to avoid our first instinct to ask questions about what we can learn here about ourselves.

What Luke is doing then is setting our Lord's ministry within the cosmic context to which it belongs. Jesus has entered into the bloodline of Adam. As the Second Man and the Last Adam he is being led on to the front line to do battle against Satan. This is a replay of Eden, but this time – as Mark points out – not in a garden where the animals were named by and obedient to Adam, and where food and beauty abounded. He was in a wilderness where there was neither food nor water, and where wild animals roamed.[3]

Jesus has come to gain victory where there has been defeat, to obey where there has been disobedience, to effect justification where there has been condemnation, to bring freedom where there has been bondage, to bring healing where there has been sickness, wholeness where there has been disintegration, reconciliation where there has been alienation, to bring blessing where there has been curse, and life where there has been death.

In short this temptation narrative tells us that what Adam failed to do, Jesus has come to do. The image of God that was marred through Adam is now being repaired through Christ; the glory from which we have fallen short is now being restored. Jesus has entered into Adam's bloodline and ours in order to do this for us!

Ultimately Christ will accomplish all this through his death and resurrection. But first he must face the enemy who defeated Adam and Eve in the Garden of Eden.

[1] Paul describes Jesus thus because (1) he is the only man since Adam who has functioned in this unique relationship to others, (2) since he succeeds where Adam failed there will be no need for any further Adams. He is the last one.

[2] See especially, but by no means exclusively, Romans 5:12-21 and 1 Corinthians 15:21-28.

[3] Mark 1:13.

The wilderness temptations constitute a kind of rerun. Where Adam failed and fell to temptation, Jesus will now be victorious. The goal is nothing less than the rescue and recreation of a new humanity of which he is the head, so that we will be restored and recreated into what we were meant to be.

Martin Luther saw this clearly, and expressed it vividly in his great hymn, *Ein feste Burg ist unser Gott* – A Mighty Fortress is our God. The version sung most commonly in the United Kingdom,[1] includes these lines:

> The ancient prince of hell
> Hath risen with purpose fell;
> Strong mail of craft and power
> He weareth in this hour;
> On earth is not his fellow.
>
> With force of arms we nothing can,
> Full soon were we down-ridden;
> But for us fights the proper Man,
> Whom God himself hath bidden.
> Ask ye, who is this same?
> Christ Jesus is His Name,
> The Lord Sabaoth's Son;
> He, and no other one,
> Shall conquer in the battle.

All this is true. But Luther is speaking about our present spiritual conflicts. Luke is inviting us to use not the present but the past tense:

> But for us *fought* the proper Man ...
> He, and no other one,
> *Has conquered* in the battle.

This is why the Gospels record that *temptation did not in the first instance come to Jesus; he marched into temptation's territory.* When we face temptation, the gospel tells us 'Run!' By contrast, led by the Holy Spirit as the director-general of his life and ministry, Jesus is told not to 'Run away, the devil is coming!' but 'Go! Enter his territory. Face him down and defeat him, for this is the task for which you have been baptized and anointed with the Spirit.'

[1] Martin Luther (1483–1546), 'A safe stronghold our God is still.' This version was translated by Thomas Carlyle (1795–1881).

So Luke does not portray Jesus as the *victim* of temptation. Rather, he is the *aggressor*. He is 'the strong Son of God' who 'goes forth to war'[1] against the powers of darkness.

Later on, Luke gives us the clue to this in Jesus' statement:

> When a strong man, fully armed, guards his own palace, his goods are safe; but when one stronger than he attacks him and overcomes him, he takes away his armour in which he trusted and divides his spoil.[2]

If we are to be set free from the destruction that Satan has wrought in our lives, his territory must first be invaded and he must be disarmed of his authority. Only then can his prisoners be set free.

This is what Jesus is doing here. He is entering the palace of the devil, the strong man armed, in order to bind him. Hence the rest of Luke's Gospel shows how, having bound the strong man armed, Jesus then

- Preaches that his kingdom has come so that people are brought to faith.

- Exorcizes demons because he has defeated their king.

- Mends lives broken by the Fall, healing the sick, giving sight to the blind, cleansing lepers, and even raising the dead.

These are all fulfilments of Old Testament prophecies of the coming of the Messianic age.[3] In different ways they give us glimpses of what the final kingdom of God is going to look like.

But first of all Jesus must create a bridgehead for the kingdom of God into a world that 'lies in the power of the evil one'.[4]

Stage one had been completed – he had become incarnate in our humanity.

Stage two had also been completed – for thirty years he had prepared for his royal priesthood and for his prophetic ministry.

---

[1] An allusion to the hymn by Reginald Heber (1783–1826), 'The Son of God goes forth to war, a kingly crown to gain.' Heber, best known for his hymn 'Holy, holy, holy', was Bishop of Calcutta in India from 1823 until his death.

[2] Luke 11:21-22.

[3] Matthew 11:4-6. See Isaiah 35:4-6; 61:1-2.

[4] 1 John 5:19.

Now stage three has commenced: having been brought on to the public stage of his messianic ministry, his first task is to deal with the devil.

The threefold temptations of Jesus, therefore, do not focus so much on his deity but upon his ministry as the Son of God in our flesh. Here we should try to watch him through the lenses of the Scriptures that describe him as the Second Man and Last Adam who has come to undo the bondage into which we were brought by the First Man and First Adam. Satan is not interested in tempting his deity, for he knows God cannot be tempted with sin. Rather he is focused on destroying the ministry that the Saviour was sent to exercise. But in the event his kingdom will be destroyed by it.

Stones into bread

In both Matthew's and Luke's accounts of the wilderness scene, the first temptation was to turn stones into bread.

> The devil said to him, 'If you are the Son of God, command this stone to become bread.'[1]

Jesus had been in the wilderness for forty days during which 'he ate nothing'. Almost gratuitously, but doubtless to underline the point, Luke adds, 'And when they were ended, he was hungry.'[2] How desperately hungry and weakened the Saviour must have felt.

Remember the big picture here. Jesus has entered the bloodline of Adam in order to begin again. But he must begin at the end, not at the beginning. He is not in a garden where he may eat the fruit of all of the trees except one. Nor does he have a human companion. He is not well-nourished by an abundance of food. No, Jesus is weakened by fasting; he feels the pangs of hunger; he is alone; he has little physical energy. This is just the time for the devil to come to him and issue his first test: 'If you are the Son of God, turn this stone into bread.'

Why is this a temptation?

Temptation is always solicitation to do what is morally wrong. But what would be *morally* wrong in Jesus' turning stones into bread? Only a few paragraphs before Luke had recorded John the Baptist saying

[1] Luke 4:3. Cf. Matthew 4:3.
[2] Luke 4:2.

that 'God is able from these stones to raise up children for Abraham.'[1]
So what could possibly be deficient in Jesus' turning stones into bread
when he was hungry? All the more so, since a few chapters later Luke
will describe how he turned bread into more bread – enough to feed
five thousand men – plus left-overs![2] What is the difference between
taking a few loaves and feeding thousands and taking one stone and
turning it into enough bread for oneself? Why should this be such a
test of Jesus?

Satan said to Jesus: '*If* you are the Son of God, command this
stone to become bread.' His words are often understood as if Satan's
purpose was to sow doubts in Jesus' mind about his divine identity.
But more probably the 'if' here has the sense of 'since'.[3] The devil is
saying to him:

> Jesus, as the Son of God you have rights. You are under no
> obligation to be hungry and thirsty, or lonely and weak.
> There is surely nothing to prevent you from exercising your
> rights as the Son of God, is there? It would not be immoral,
> for all the stones in the world are your creation. Every loaf
> of bread is dependent upon your providential upholding
> of the universe. There cannot possibly be anything wrong
> if you – the Son of God – turn stone into bread to satisfy
> your hunger.

Is there a flaw in Satan's logic? It wouldn't be *immoral*, would it?

Do you see what the devil is doing? He is intensely subtle. He is
addressing Jesus as the Son of God, and suggesting he use his inalien-
able rights. But it is not because he has any need for himself as the

---

[1] Luke 3:8.

[2] Luke 9:10-17.

[3] This is a common, but not always understood, meaning of 'if', and carries the
sense of '*Since this is so*, it follows that …' In technical grammar it is a 'first class conditional' assuming the truth of the statement for the sake of argument. John Newton's hymn 'Glorious things of Thee are spoken, Zion city of our God' provides a
good example: 'Saviour, *if* of Zion's city I through grace a member am, Let the world
deride or pity, I will glory in Thy Name.' In one congregation to which we belonged
someone had systematically scored out the word 'if' in the hymn-book and replaced
it with the word 'since'. But he (or she) probably did not realize that this was an
example of the first class conditional. Or perhaps, to put the defacing in a better
light, they simply wanted to make sure everybody singing the hymn realized it!

Son of God that Jesus is in the wilderness. He is there as the Second *Man*. Where Adam became disobedient by taking and eating, Jesus means to be obedient by not taking and by not eating. Only thus can he be 'Adam in reverse' undoing what the First Man did and doing what he failed to do.

Thus the devil was attempting to blind-side Jesus to his calling. Although he is in the form of God so that equality with God is not something that he needs to grasp, his present calling is to humble himself as a servant and become obedient to the point of death, even death on a cross.[1] The real issue is whether he is going to follow through on this covenant with his Father and, with the help of the Holy Spirit, endure the state of humiliation.

How devilish of Satan to seek to take advantage of Jesus' humanity in all its physical weakness and frailty – presumably even to the point of feeling faint.

In such a weakened condition we do not always think clearly. So Satan is also attacking Jesus' mind and his understanding of his ministry. 'Let's focus on your deity. There's surely nothing wrong with your turning this stone into bread, since you are the Son of God.'

Notice how Jesus resists. Notice especially his emphasis: '*Man* shall not live by bread alone …' It is a defence against the attack that began 'You are the Son of God, so … .' Jesus does not lose sight of his vocation. Rather he responds:

> I have not come into this world to exercise my prerogatives … I am here *for man* and therefore I must live *as man*. Further, my calling is to experience humiliation and weakness and rejection and to live not by the satisfaction of my needs but by every word that proceeds from the mouth of God. I will obey his word even to the point of death, even if that means death on a cross, rather than turn a stone into bread to alleviate my hunger and relieve myself of my suffering servant status!

What a reversal this was of events in the Garden of Eden! Food was an issue there too, and a source of temptation. The serpent said to Eve (and by implication to Adam 'who was with her'[2]): 'Eat and you will

---

[1] See Philippians 2:5-8.
[2] Genesis 3:6.

not surely die but live as gods.' Now he comes to the Messiah and says, 'Eat like the Son of God you are, or you will surely die as a man.' This is what makes Jesus' response so powerful. He says,

> Unlike Adam, I will not fall to your temptation to be as God (although I am!); for I have come as man to restore man. Therefore I say to you, 'As *man* I shall not live by turning a stone into bread to put into my mouth, but by every word that comes from the mouth of God.'

It is a stunning resistance of the evil one. Where Adam sought *exaltation*, Jesus embraced *humiliation*. Of course, this is the whole point. What lies behind each and all of the devil's strategies is his attempt to distort Jesus' commitment to his ministry and to divert him from the way of humiliation.

But there are still two temptations left to endure.

All this world's kingdoms

Satan now comes and shows Jesus the kingdoms of this world in a moment of time, and says to him, 'To you I will give all this authority and their glory, for it has been delivered to me … If you, then, will worship me, it will all be yours.'[1]

Now, if you fail with your first temptation, don't you usually tighten the screws in the second temptation? But how is this a stronger temptation? Isn't it too obvious to be one? Why did the devil think he could possibly gain any traction in this way?

Would this be a temptation to you? Yes, we are weak Christians. But if Satan said, 'I'll give you the kingdoms of this world', wouldn't you simply laugh him off? That's no real temptation to you. Whatever your faults you are not that kind of megalomaniac. You have never seriously wanted to rule the world! Why then would this be a temptation to the meek and lowly Jesus? Why did Jesus not shrug it off and say, 'Your first effort was better than this one!'

Yet this must have been a very powerful temptation. Otherwise why would the devil have attempted it?

Satan is a liar, but there is an important element of truth in what he claims to be able to give Jesus here. The world is under his authority.

[1] Luke 4:6-7.

He is 'the god of this world [age]';[1] 'the whole world lies in the power of the evil one'.[2] Now he is offering back to Jesus what was forfeited by Adam (to whom God had originally entrusted this dominion[3]). Jesus can have what he had come into the world to gain. And he can have it all without the cross!

That is why this is a very real temptation.

We may tempt you with things that are of no interest to you. If you will quietly cover up my wrong we will fly you to Scotland and treat you to rounds of golf on the Championship Course at Carnoustie and on the Old Course at St Andrews. You will walk on the same turf on which Ben Hogan and Jack Nicklaus won The Open Championship. But you have no interest in golf. So our temptation has no power to entice you. But if you love golf – well, that gives our tempting offer a great deal of traction!

So here again, behind the narrative of the temptation in the wilderness lies the creation account and especially Genesis 1:26-28. God created Adam to have dominion over all creation and to extend his rule to the ends of the earth. He was given a garden to begin with,[4] and a sacred task to take care of it[5] and to expand it (presumably with his descendants) until its borders overflowed into the whole earth.

But Adam lost both the plan for his life and his place in the garden. The world over which he was king shared the consequences with him.[6] His dominion was usurped.

But God gave our first parents a promise of recovery – a promise that ultimately leads to Jesus.

---

[1] 2 Corinthians 4:4.

[2] 1 John 5:19.

[3] Genesis 1:28.

[4] The fact that God 'planted a garden in Eden, in the east, and there he put the man whom he had formed' (Genesis 2:8) implies that not all the earth was garden. Adam's dominion or royal role is to be a miniature creator whose Father has given him a start and encourages him to finish the task of 'gardening' the whole earth for his glory.

[5] Genesis 2:15. The language here is reminiscent of the vocabulary used for the task of the priests to guard the sanctuary. Numbers 1:53; 3:7, 8, 32; 8:26; 18:2-5.

[6] Genesis 3:17-19.

• A champion would emerge from the seed of Eve. He would engage in conflict with and defeat the serpent.[1]

• Later this promise was narrowed down to the seed of Abraham in particular, in whom 'all the families of the earth shall be blessed'.[2]

• The promise of the Father to the Son, recorded in Psalm 2:8, further described what this would mean: 'Ask of me, and I will make the nations your heritage.'

• Daniel's vision of the Son of Man receiving the kingdom from the Ancient of Days and sharing it with his people made this even clearer.[3]

• The Book of Revelation describes the ultimate fulfilment of the promise: 'The kingdom of this world has become the kingdom of our Lord and of his Christ, and he shall reign forever and ever.'[4]

This is what the Son of God came into the world to accomplish. Yes, he came to forgive our sins. But the forgiveness of sins was also a means to the creation of a new humanity and the restoration of the created order. That is why after his death and resurrection and in view of his ascension to the throne of God, Jesus announced, 'All *authority* [or *dominion*] in heaven and on earth has been given to me.'[5] What was lost by Adam has now been restored in Christ.

Now when we set the devil's temptation within this context we see that he is saying:

> Haven't you come into the world for this – to gain authority over the kingdoms of this world? You can have them here and now – without the dark shadow of a cross hanging over you for the rest of your life. Think of it: you will never have to experience feeling forsaken by God; you will not have to go out into the dark on your own. Take this other way I am offering to you. It will mean no more suffering. It will

---

[1] Genesis 3:15.
[2] Genesis 12:3.
[3] Daniel 7:13-14, 27.
[4] Revelation 11:15.
[5] Matthew 28:18.

mean no more shame. It will mean no more pain. You will
have everything that you have desired to have, plus you will
avoid the cross. All you need to do is to kneel and ask me.

Here also was a powerful appeal to one of Jesus' deepest instincts.

Here was a way of ending forever the terrible weakness that must
have racked Jesus' humanity. There need be no more swimming
against the tide.

Here was a real test.

But Jesus both saw through the subtle nature of the temptation and
resisted it with every fibre of his being. Notice his response:

> Yes, Satan. But I see through your words. I will not be
> deceived by your subtlety. You are asking me to gain what
> Adam lost by doing the very thing that Adam did – by
> listening to your voice rather than God's voice.

This explains the significance of our Lord's response, 'It is written,
"You shall worship the Lord your God [notice the way this is further
explained] and him *only* – [notice the words] – you shall *serve*.'[1]

Why are these words so significant? Because they reflect the very
passages that we have seen were the lenses through which the Lord
Jesus viewed his whole life and ministry. In Isaiah's prophecies the
Servant of the Lord emerges as one who will be submissive to his
heavenly Father's will and way, even though that means becoming the
Suffering Servant, tasting humiliation, alienation, desolation, and even
a sense of isolation from God. Jesus is saying to the devil:

> I did indeed come into this world to regain all its kingdoms.
> But I did so knowing that this could be done only by a
> humble, obedient, crucified servant. Therefore before God
> my Father alone will I bow.

Here we have a kind of foretaste of what Paul says Christ will do
when he returns at the end of history. He will bring a reconstituted,
transformed cosmos and a redeemed people into the presence of his
Father, and bow before him as he offers back to God what Adam was
originally called to bring to him:

---

[1] Deuteronomy 6:13.

When all things are subjected to him, then the Son himself
will also be subjected to him who put all things in subjection
under him, that God may be all in all.[1]

The context in which Paul wrote these words makes it clear that
he was not speaking *ontologically* here, as though the Divine Son was
a subordinate deity to the Divine Father. He was thinking *economically*.[2] It is as the Second Man and the Last Adam who has fulfilled
everything prophesied of him that the Son Incarnate will bow as
our representative before his heavenly Father and say, 'Father, I have
done it all. I have paid for it, restored it, transferred it. And now I am
bringing it to you. It is my love gift to you.' Then the Second Man,
the Last Adam, Jesus will have undone all that Adam did, and done
what Adam failed to do. And then God will be all in all.

Although hungry, and thirsty, and experiencing all the physical and
mental side-effects of six weeks of fasting, loneliness, cold and heat,
the Lord Jesus will yield in nothing to the devil in order to bring in
that glorious day!

This, however, still leaves the final temptation.

Trust the angels?

The third temptation, in Luke's record, describes how the devil
transported Jesus to the pinnacle of the temple and said to him, 'If
you are the Son of God, throw yourself down from here.'[3]

The order in which Luke records the temptations differs from
Matthew's, which is: (1) 'Turn stones into bread'; (2) 'Jump down
from the temple pinnacle'; and (3) 'The kingdoms of this world will
be yours if you will just bow down before me.'

Both authors seem more concerned to set the significance of the
temptations in the context of their particular narratives than they are
with their original chronological sequence.

[1] 1 Corinthians 15:28.
[2] Ontologically, *i.e.* in terms of his divine being; economically, *i.e.* in terms of his
ministry in our human nature.
[3] Luke 4:9. Notice that the devil returns to his appeal to Jesus as 'the Son of God',
which had been subtly absent from the middle temptation – after all, why would
he remind Jesus that he was the Son of God, and then invite him to bow before the
god of this age?

It is easy to see how the temptations move to a climax in Matthew's account, and fit into his over-arching pattern. His Gospel is book-ended at the beginning by wise men *from the nations* coming to the infant Christ and then at the end with the risen Christ sending his disciples *to the nations*.[1] Hence the climactic temptation relates to the nations.

But Luke is describing the temptations from a different perspective. Whatever the precise element in the architecture of the Jerusalem temple is meant by 'the pinnacle', Luke sees it as the highest point in Jerusalem, the city of God, and in that sense the centre of the cosmos. The implication is that the devil is saying to Jesus,

> Since you are the Son of God, jump down from the top of the temple. God has promised that his angels will protect you! Show the whole cosmos that you trust his word and they will undoubtedly flock to follow you. We both know that it is written:
>
>> 'He will command his angels concerning you
>> to guard you.'
>
> and
>
>> 'On their hands they will bear you up
>> lest you strike your foot against a stone.'[2]
>
> So, Jesus, jump. One major sign to the world that you trust God to guard you will be enough to bring it to bow before you!

Now what is wrong with that? If at creation the morning stars could sing together; if one day the trees will clap their hands for joy,[3] is there anything conceivably wrong with the Son of God showing his trust in his servants the angels in his heavenly Father's house? What could possibly be wrong with that? He is, after all, the Son of God!

But that is the issue, isn't it? He is the Son of God, but he has come to act as man for man. He has come into the world to assume *our* weakness and *our* frailty and *our* shame and *our* humiliation. He has not come in order to play in the world that he created, but in order to save it at great cost to himself.

[1] See Matthew 2:1-12 and 28:18-20.
[2] The quotations are from Psalm 91:11-12.
[3] Job 38:7; Isaiah 55:12.

Satan is back to his old tactics again here, seeking to divert Jesus from his mission as the Suffering Servant to his rights as the Son of God. Why shouldn't the Son of God play in the temple precincts? It's his Father's house!

But there is more.

The sword of the Spirit

The nature of these temptations is most clearly disclosed by the way our Lord responds to them. Thus Jesus' quotation from Deuteronomy 6:16: 'You shall not put the Lord your God to the test' must be a direct negation of the specific character of the third temptation.

So how would jumping from the pinnacle of the temple 'test' God?[1]

Until now Jesus was the one who had been quoting Scripture to the devil.[2] Now the devil is quoting Scripture back at Jesus! It is as if he is saying, 'You are the one who wants to trust God's word; well show that you really trust it. Jump! You are the king of the angels. You don't doubt that they will catch you … Or do you?'

Do you detect here an accent reminiscent of Eden?

Once again Satan is taking God's word and distorting it.[3] Now he is tempting Jesus to test God – that is if he is sure God really does care for him and wants no harm to come to him. There is surely an echo here of the serpent's innuendoes to Eve and through her to Adam in the Garden of Eden.

But there is something else. Think of the impact of this spectacle to which the devil tempts Jesus! There would be no doubt left in anyone's mind that he really was the Son of God. Everyone would follow him!

Yet notice the essence of our Lord's response:

> Yes, Satan, you have quoted very fine Scripture. But you have twisted it by failing to compare Scripture with Scripture. You are tempting the Messiah to gain a people who will follow him by one spectacular act of glorious trust in one of the promises of God instead of by the long, slowly passing

[1] The meaning of these words is that Jesus will not test his Father, *not* that since he, Jesus, is God, the devil should not be testing him. *That* would hardly be adequate defence when in fact the devil *was* testing him.

[2] In response to the first temptation he had quoted from Deuteronomy 8:3; in response to the second from Deuteronomy 6:13.

[3] See Genesis 3:1, 4, where he had done the same thing.

years of humiliation, rejection, alienation, condemnation, crucifixion and death. But that is the only means by which sinners can be saved.

You are asking me to put God to the test by abandoning his salvation plan and creating my own. In essence you are asking me to do what the Israelites did during the wilderness wanderings – when at Massah 'they tested the Lord by saying, "Is the Lord among us or not?"'[1] When they were hungry and thirsty they demanded that God show them his supernatural power rather than obey his word. But I will not thus put God to the test. He has shown me the pathway, and from his path I refuse to deviate.

And so Jesus says, 'You shall not tempt the Lord your God.' He yields himself, whatever the cost, to the purposes of his heavenly Father. Where Adam (and Israel after him) had failed and fallen, Jesus obeyed and stood against all the wiles of the devil.

Suffering to glory

At the end of Luke's Gospel, in his record of the events of Easter Day, he notes that on two separate occasions,[2] Jesus explained the divine pattern to his disciples:

It was necessary for the Messiah to enter into his sufferings in order that the way might be cleared for him to enter into his glory.

My Father said to me, 'You are my Son. But you have come here to serve as the Suffering Servant. You are the Messiah, but only by a lifetime of obedience and by undergoing the curse of the cross can you undo Adam's disobedience. You are indeed my Son, and I love you, but only by stooping down low to the death of the cross in the place of sinners can you bring restoration where Adam brought condemnation. So do not be surprised that the pathway to glory – and the only way in which I will bring you to glory – is by the way of humiliation.'

Thus Jesus resisted the three-pronged attack of the devil, and defeated him on his own territory. He unmasked him. The devil

[1] Exodus 17:7.
[2] See Luke 24:26 and 46.

appealed to Jesus' sense of taste and sight, just as he had done with Adam and Eve. But unlike them, Jesus had appealed to God's word and to how he heard it. He saw through the devil's tactics when he was offered victory by short-term means. He was committed to long-term faithfulness. He defeated the devil who sought to distract him from the cross. Here, then, Jesus exposes the devil for what he really is behind his mask: the enemy of God, and at the same time the enemy of humanity.

Yes, there is a great deal we can learn about how to respond to temptation from the temptations of Jesus. But that is not Luke's point. He wants us to fix our eyes on Jesus.

John Henry Newman got this right, when he wrote:

> O loving wisdom of our God!
>   When all was sin and shame,
> A second Adam to the fight
>   And to the rescue came.
>
> O wisest love! that flesh and blood,
>   That did in Adam fail,
> Should strive afresh against the foe,
>   Should strive and should prevail.[1]

---

[1] John Henry Newman (1801–90), from the hymn 'Praise to the Holiest in the height' which in turn is part of his poem *The Dream of Gerontius* which was set to music by Edward Elgar in 1900 and is often regarded as one of his finest works. Newman's Roman Catholicism permeates parts of the poem, including 'Praise to the Holiest in the height.' That notwithstanding these two verses give powerful expression to biblical theology.

4. The Mountain – *Transfiguration*

Who is He whose clothes now shine
On the mountain top He climbed?

'Tis the Lord! O wondrous story!
'Tis the Lord! the King of glory!
At His feet we humbly fall;
Crown Him, Crown Him Lord of all.

Luke 9:28-36

Now about eight days after these sayings he took with him Peter and John and James and went up on the mountain to pray. ²⁹ And as he was praying, the appearance of his face was altered, and his clothing became dazzling white. ³⁰ And behold, two men were talking with him, Moses and Elijah, ³¹ who appeared in glory and spoke of his departure, which he was about to accomplish at Jerusalem. ³² Now Peter and those who were with him were heavy with sleep, but when they became fully awake they saw his glory and the two men who stood with him. ³³ And as the men were parting from him, Peter said to Jesus, 'Master, it is good that we are here. Let us make three tents, one for you and one for Moses and one for Elijah' – not knowing what he said. ³⁴ As he was saying these things, a cloud came and overshadowed them, and they were afraid as they entered the cloud. ³⁵ And a voice came out of the cloud, saying, 'This is my Son, my Chosen One; listen to him!' ³⁶ And when the voice had spoken, Jesus was found alone. And they kept silent and told no one in those days anything of what they had seen.

I N our school days in the United Kingdom religious instruction was a standard element in education. But it sometimes amounted to no more than memorizing passages of Scripture – all, of course, in the Authorised (King James) Version of the Bible.

At the time it all seemed rather tedious. But the passages have stuck, none more so than Isaiah chapter 53. Our elementary teacher did not know that this passage – the fourth of the Servant Songs – actually begins in Isaiah 52. But nonetheless even a child could be fascinated by one of the most striking statements in this ancient prophecy about the coming Saviour:

> He had no form or majesty that we should look at him,
> And no beauty that we should desire him.[1]

Has it ever struck you as remarkable that we have four pen portraits of Jesus and yet we have no real idea what he looked like? There is not a word in the Gospels about his appearance. History gives us one description of the Apostle Paul, but it is little more than what we might have imagined him to be![2] But we have none of Jesus. Would we have passed him by in the street without recognizing him?

Yet for a brief moment all this changed. Jesus' appearance was dramatically transformed in an event usually described as 'the Transfiguration':

> Now about eight days after these sayings he took with him
> Peter and John and James and went up on the mountain to

[1] Isaiah 53:2. In the AV (KJV): 'he hath no form nor comeliness; and when we shall see him there is no beauty that we should desire him'.

[2] It is found in the apocryphal and hagiographical work *The Acts of Paul and Thecla* II. 3 (dated probably around the latter part of the second century): 'he was a man of middling size, and his hair was scanty, and his legs were a little crooked, and his knees were projecting, and he had large [or blue] eyes and his eyebrows met, and his nose was somewhat long, and he was full of grace and mercy; at one time he seemed like a man, and at another time he seemed like an angel.'

pray. And as he was praying, the appearance of his face was altered, and his clothing became dazzling white.[1]

All of the first three Gospels see this unique event as a central point in their narratives, and as a hinge and turning point in Jesus' life.

Simon Peter had recently confessed Jesus as the Christ, the Son of the living God. Jesus had responded by beginning to teach the disciples what this meant – the suffering and death of the cross and the triumph of the resurrection, all taking place at Jerusalem. He had then spoken to them about the implications of all this for his followers. Nobody could be his disciple without taking up the cross and following him.[2] Christians must be able – in Paul's words – to say: 'Far be it from me to boast except in the cross of our Lord Jesus Christ by which the world has been crucified to me, and I to the world.'[3]

Thereafter Jesus 'set his face to go to Jerusalem'.[4]

So this is clearly a point of no return. The die was cast. Perhaps this was the reason Jesus comforted his disciples with the assurance that he would rise from the dead,[5] and then promised them: 'there are some standing here who will not taste death until they see the kingdom of God'.[6]

The kingdom

The kingdom of God is his reign and dominion in this world. It became present in Jesus himself since he is the King in the kingdom. And where he is, there the kingdom is present.

But Jesus ushered in his kingdom in stages. He had already created a bridgehead for it in the world by victory over the devil in the wilderness. He preached about this kingdom.[7] Because of the ministry that followed he could say, 'The kingdom of God is in the midst of you.'[8]

---

[1] Luke 9:28-9.
[2] Luke 9:18-27.
[3] Galatians 6:14.
[4] Luke 9:51.
[5] Luke 9:22.
[6] Luke 9:27. The reference is probably to the kingdom coming through his death, resurrection, ascension and the outpouring of the Spirit on the Day of Pentecost.
[7] Matthew 4:17, 23.
[8] Luke 17:21.

He talked about people belonging to the kingdom, and described what they were like.[1]

This kingdom was going to be further manifested in his death and resurrection through which he would conquer sin and death. Following his ascension to the right hand of God, a further development would take place on the day of Pentecost. Then his reign began to spread in a multi-national manner.

But Christ's kingdom is still to come in its consummate form, according to the New Testament, when he returns. For then: 'the kingdom of the world' will have become 'the kingdom of our Lord and of his Christ, and he shall reign forever and ever'.[2]

So while Jesus placed great emphasis on the costliness of being his follower, on the other hand he taught his disciples that the kingdom of grace ushered in by the cross was destined to be the kingdom of glory to be ushered in by his return. And on this never-to-be-forgotten day when he was transfigured, some of his disciples were given a glimpse into that momentous event.

The three

Jesus took only three of his disciples with him as witnesses: Peter, James, and John.

But why these three? Why not Andrew, or Philip? And would it not have been a major help to Thomas to have been there?

In some sense they were Jesus' 'inner circle'. We know that they had been with him like this at least once before to witness the raising of Jairus' daughter.[3] Perhaps he was already thinking forward and realizing that he would want these same three men to be close to him on the night of his passion.[4] Was it because he knew they would witness his humiliation that he wanted them especially to see the real truth about him?

Whatever the reason, as Jesus was praying his face seemed to change, and his clothes too. A brilliance overtook them. Moses and Elijah appeared, as if through a fold in heaven, and discussed Jesus'

[1] Matthew 5:1-20.
[2] Revelation 11:15.
[3] Luke 8:40-56.
[4] Mark 14:33.

death. The experience seems to have exhausted the three disciples both physically and emotionally. How could we otherwise explain that in the aftermath of this vision they became 'heavy with sleep'?

There are at least four clues in the Transfiguration narrative that help us to understand its significance.

Alteration

Jesus' appearance was altered. We call it by its traditional name: 'the Transfiguration'. That is not Luke's title. He simply says that 'the appearance of his face was altered, and his clothing became dazzling white'.[1]

Jesus was praying at the time.

But this did not usually happen when Jesus prayed with his disciples.

On this occasion it did.

We are given neither explanation nor interpretation. However Luke gives us some clues.

At one level we are quite accustomed to people's appearance changing. We see a colleague on Monday morning and say, 'You are *looking* a bit glum today.' Or we say to someone else on Friday evening, 'You *look* in good spirits tonight!' We can often tell when friends are in love, or depressed, or impatient, simply by looking at their faces. We speak of people whose smile can 'light up' an entire room. Somehow our inner disposition comes to the surface, involuntarily. Others see it.

That may be a clue to what happened to Jesus. But what is being described here goes far beyond it. A closer analogy might be the way the face of Moses shone when he met with God on Mount Sinai.[2] When he emerged from the presence of God his skin seemed to be filled with light – as though being in the presence of God had a physical impact on him – as if he had looked on the face of God and now his own face glowed as a reflection of his glory. As the moon reflects the light of the sun, so Moses' face reflected the God who dwells in unapproachable light. He 'glowed' as a result of the intimacy of fellowship he enjoyed 'face to face' with God.[3]

[1] Luke 9:29.
[2] See Exodus 34:29-35.
[3] Exodus 33:11.

Luke had recorded something similar earlier in his Gospel. When the angelic announcement of the birth of Christ was made to the Bethlehem shepherds, 'the glory of the Lord shone around them'.[1]

Sometimes standing at the church door on a Sunday evening, greeting people at the end of the Lord's Day – people who have been gazing on the face of the Lord in Scripture – we ourselves have seen faces glowing, some with burdens relieved, others with fresh insight into their lives, all with a sense that they have shared David's experience of gazing on 'the beauty of the Lord'.[2] The blessing of the Lord has been pronounced on them: 'The Lord make his face to shine upon you ... the Lord lift up his countenance upon you and give you peace.'[3] There is a 'glow' of satisfaction. They do not see it with the naked eye, but they may comment on what they have experienced by saying, 'That was glorious tonight!' Sometimes, not always!

But these experiences also pale by comparison with what the disciples saw. Peter said that they were 'eyewitnesses of his majesty'. He describes what happened as Jesus received 'honour and glory from God'.[4] John who says that Jesus was always 'face to face with God', bathed from all eternity in his Father's love, also said that 'we have seen his glory, glory as of the only Son from the Father, full of grace and truth'. He too was an eyewitness of his glory.[5]

Conversation

Luke describes what the disciples saw. But this was not a wordless event. They also overheard a conversation among Jesus, Moses and Elijah. What a moment this must have been! They had climbed the mountain to a prayer meeting.[6] They hardly expected Moses and Elijah to be present! Two of the greatest of the Old Testament saints had been allowed, as it were, an hour to leave the confines of the city of God, the glory of the presence of God, and come and sit with Jesus on top of a mountain.

---

[1] Luke 2:9.
[2] Psalm 27:4.
[3] Numbers 6:25-26.
[4] 2 Peter 1:16-17.
[5] John 1:14.
[6] Luke 9:28.

Both men had met with God before on a mountain.[1] But why were they here on this occasion? And why these two men in particular?

Moses and Elijah were the two great representative figures of the Old Testament. It was as if the disciples were seeing a *tableau* in which the Law and the Prophets were present to bear witness to their fulfilment in Jesus.

They had come to talk with Jesus about 'the departure which he was about to accomplish at Jerusalem'.[2] Luke chose his vocabulary with obvious care. 'Departure' is the Greek word *exodus*. The implication is unmissable. The geographical Exodus from Egypt had been a pointer to a greater Exodus. However this greater Exodus would not be from physical bondage in Egypt under the dominion of a cruel and oppressive Pharaoh – but from a deeper oppression under sin, Satan, and death. The miracle of the Exodus in which God called his son Israel from Egypt was a dramatic type of what God was planning to do in his Son![3]

What would we give to have been present to overhear that conversation? How did the discussion go? Did Jesus do most of the talking? Did he speak about how the sacrifice of the Passover lamb saving the firstborn sons of Israel from the judgment of the angel of death was a picture of how he himself would be both Passover Lamb and Firstborn Son? It must, surely, have been similar to the conversation he had on Easter Day with the two disciples on the road to Emmaus. Then Jesus took Cleopas and his companion through the Law of Moses and all of the Prophets and showed them how these sacred writings pointed towards his death and resurrection. Truly it was 'necessary that the Christ should suffer … and enter into his glory'.[4]

Earlier Peter had found this teaching intolerable, and had resisted it.[5] But here Jesus was showing him that there was no other pathway to glory than by way of the cross. Moses and Elijah were the two witnesses in whose mouths this truth was established.[6]

[1] Exodus 19:20; 1 Kings 19:8.

[2] Luke 9:31.

[3] A notion already present in the prophecy of Hosea. See Hosea 11:1 and Matthew 2:15.

[4] Luke 24:26.

[5] Matthew 16:21-23.

[6] See Deuteronomy 17:6; 19:15 for the principle.

Reaction

There was a whole series of reactions to what happened.

The first was that Peter, James and John fell asleep. Their behaviour seems irresponsible, and we are naturally critical of them. They fell asleep again in the Garden of Gethsemane. But it was almost certainly night time in Gethsemane. They were tired and frightened. What overpowered them here? Perhaps the stunning way in which they were given confirmation that their Master was going to be crucified. Certainly, however, it was the manifestation of the glory of God they had just witnessed.

It should not surprise us that they were overwhelmed. We have too superficial a view of the *physical* impact of the presence of God. Whenever there is a special manifestation of God's glory in Scripture the impact is felt physically. Isaiah felt undone.[1] In the upper room the Apostle John had been able to lean on the Lord Jesus. But when he saw him in his exalted glory he 'fell at his feet as though dead'.[2] It was the same on the Mount of Transfiguration. Christ's glory is overwhelming, even exhausting.

When Peter awakens, he characteristically speaks without really thinking: 'It is good for us to be here', he says.

'For *us*'?

Had Peter nothing to say about Jesus? Didn't he realize that this was not about him? Will he never forget about himself? Can he not keep his gaze fixed on the Lord Jesus?

Poor Peter, he is still taken up with how things affect him. Yes, it was good for him to be there. But that is not the first thought that should enter your mind when you have seen the glory of Jesus Christ.

But then Peter has another foolish thought: 'This has been so good, let's stay here. Let's build some huts; one for you, one for Moses, and another for Elijah.'[3]

But Moses and Elijah were human beings. Peter has just seen the glory of Jesus Christ! And now he is talking about putting up tents? Does he want simply to prolong the bliss? Or is what he has heard

[1] Isaiah 6:5.
[2] Revelation 1:17.
[3] Luke 9:33.

beginning to register? Is there a little voice at the back of his mind that says, 'Down the mountain lies the way to the cross of shame and to the exposing of your sinful heart, and the coming pain of God's grace taking hold of you and bringing you to a deeper experience of repentance and faith, and then remaking you. Stay here!'?

This is why something else happens.

Proclamation

God the Father intervenes in two ways.

First a cloud comes down. Clouds on mountain summits are not unusual. The appearance of one might understandably have produced a nervousness about the journey back down the mountain. But this cloud filled them with a sense of dread. It was the glory cloud of the presence of God.

We have met this cloud before in the biblical narrative. It is the cloud in which God manifested his presence during the Exodus wanderings.[1] It is the same cloud that Moses entered when he met with God on Sinai;[2] the same cloud that covered the tabernacle;[3] the same cloud that filled Solomon's temple.[4] It is the *Shekinah* – the glory cloud of the presence of God coming down. That is why they were 'afraid'.[5]

Again Luke seems to have been very deliberate in his choice of words. Here he uses the same verb he had earlier used about the Holy Spirit *overshadowing* Mary when he came to empower her at the conception of the Lord Jesus.[6] Was the darkness at Calvary also a manifestation of this same cloud? It is the physical expression of God's presence in space and time inexorably fulfilling his purposes.

But here God not only comes. He speaks. His words are both a rebuke and a revelation: 'This is my Son, this is my Chosen One; listen to him!'[7]

Like the words spoken at Jesus' baptism these words are an echo of several Old Testament passages.

[1] Exodus 13:21-2.
[2] Exodus 24:15-18.
[3] Numbers 9:15-22.
[4] 1 Kings 8:10-11.
[5] Luke 9:34.
[6] Luke 1:35, the only other occurrence of the verb in Luke's Gospel.
[7] Luke 9:35.

They echo the words of Moses that God would raise up a prophet like him, to whom people should listen.

Perhaps they also echo the words of the second Psalm about God setting his Son as king on his holy hill and urging men and women to 'kiss the Son', that is to yield to him and entrust their lives to him.[1]

'When the voice had spoken, Jesus was found alone.'[2] Jesus … alone. Here the medium really is the message. It is one more *tableau* depiction of how the Christian life is to be lived. Yes, we read Moses and the Prophets (Elijah). But we misread them unless we see that they are pointing to someone else – to Jesus – and summoning us to trust in him. For the whole of the Christian life in a sense can be reduced to this: if we are going to live it well and to the glory of God, then Jesus alone must be the one who fills our horizon.

We are all too much like Peter. We talk too much. We listen far too little. Especially when it comes to Christ. But here, on the Mount of Transfiguration something significant happened to these three men. For a prolonged period after their experience they did not mention what they had seen. Luke omits a detail here that we find in Matthew and Mark: it was Jesus who told them not to share with others what they had seen until after his resurrection.[3] They were wise enough to 'listen to him'.

How different it often is today. There is so much kudos in being able to claim an unusual (and usually 'superior') spiritual experience – alas! But when you meet Christ in this way you do not want to talk about it. You are too much in awe of who he is to disclose what you have experienced. Why? Because the moment you disclose it your experience becomes fodder – for people to talk about you rather than about him. And so people say – 'Have you heard about So and So?' 'Have you read the book?' 'What do you think about this boy's experience?' 'Have you heard what happened to this woman?' It is all about this man, or that boy, or this girl, or that woman. It has ceased to be about the Lord Jesus Christ. But when you have really encountered the Lord of glory two things are inevitable accompaniments. One, you fall silent. You do not want to talk much about yourself. Two, you want to think and speak more of him.

[1] Deuteronomy 18:15-19; Psalm 2:1-12.
[2] Luke 9:36.
[3] See Matthew 17:9 and Mark 9:9.

So here is this marvellous event. We can only scrape its surface. But even this is a start.

There is a further simple but important lesson for us to learn here. If we see Jesus as he really is, then it leaves an indelible mark on our lives. We will have something in common with Jacob after he had met with the angel of God and had wrestled a blessing from him. A limp. The mark of the humbled.[1]

We have a thousand different needs. But at the end of the day, there is only one need. The satisfying of this one need will relegate all our other needs to the margins. It is to see the glory of the Lord Jesus Christ, and to know that 'he is able to save to the uttermost those who draw near to God through him'.[2]

Have you caught sight of him yet, and listened to him? The Transfiguration shows you who Jesus really is: he is the one who suffered for our sins and entered the glory that was his with the Father before the world began.[3] Will you not bow down and worship him in faith?

Both John and Peter wrote of the lasting impression made on them by the Transfiguration:

> We have seen his glory, glory as of the only Son from the Father, full of grace and truth.[4]

> We were eye witnesses of his majesty. For when he received honour and glory from God the Father, and the voice was borne to him by the Majestic Glory, 'This is my beloved Son, with whom I am well pleased,' we ourselves heard this very voice borne from heaven, for we were with him on the holy mountain.[5]

So let us lay down in the dust all our own glory, and listen to him.

---

[1] Genesis 32:22-32.
[2] Hebrews 7:25.
[3] John 17:24.
[4] John 1:14.
[5] 2 Peter 1:16-18.

5. The Garden – *Decision*

Lo! at midnight, who is He
Prays in dark Gethsemane?

'Tis the Lord! O wondrous story!
'Tis the Lord! the King of glory!
At His feet we humbly fall;
Crown Him, Crown Him Lord of all.

Matthew 26:36-46

Then Jesus went with them to a place called Gethsemane, and he said to his disciples, 'Sit here, while I go over there and pray.' [37] And taking with him Peter and the two sons of Zebedee, he began to be sorrowful and troubled. [38] Then he said to them, 'My soul is very sorrowful, even to death; remain here, and watch with me.' [39] And going a little farther he fell on his face and prayed, saying, 'My Father, if it be possible, let this cup pass from me; nevertheless, not as I will, but as you will.' [40] And he came to the disciples and found them sleeping. And he said to Peter, 'So, could you not watch with me one hour? [41] Watch and pray that you may not enter into temptation. The spirit indeed is willing, but the flesh is weak.' [42] Again, for the second time, he went away and prayed, 'My Father, if this cannot pass unless I drink it, your will be done.' [43] And again he came and found them sleeping, for their eyes were heavy. [44] So, leaving them again, he went away and prayed for the third time, saying the same words again. [45] Then he came to the disciples and said to them, 'Sleep and take your rest later on. See, the hour is at hand, and the Son of Man is betrayed into the hands of sinners. [46] Rise, let us be going; see, my betrayer is at hand.'

IT is the evening before the Crucifixion. Jesus walks across the Kidron valley and into the Garden of Gethsemane. This is holy ground; it is the antechamber to Calvary. Here we see our Lord coming face to face with the full reality of being the Suffering Servant, the curse-bearer taking the place of sinners like ourselves.

This is a decisive moment.

The story of the human race began in a garden. Now we are back in a garden. In the Garden of Eden the first Adam sinned and fell. Now in the Garden of Gethsemane the last Adam faces the final test of his obedience.

For a moment let us follow him. Let us sit alongside Peter and James and John, and watch Jesus go a little further, a stone's throw according to one of the Gospel writers.[1] His burden presses him to the ground and he engages in intense, personal intercession with his heavenly Father.

Our Lord is sensing that the day is about to dawn when he will walk the *Via Dolorosa*. He can see the hill called Golgotha in his mind's eye. The reality will only be worse than what he presently senses here in the garden. Here he can still call God 'My Father'.[2]

Progressive knowledge, progressive obedience

We should not think that Jesus acquired information about his future all at once. Throughout the whole course of his life he surely 'increased in wisdom and in stature and in favour with God and man'.[3] Think of him reading the Scriptures, meditating long and hard on particular passages of the Old Testament, coming to terms with what it would mean to be the Servant of the Lord. Initially, as a young boy, Joseph and Mary would be there with him as he did so, perhaps trying to

[1] Luke 22:41.
[2] Matthew 26:39, 42; cf. 27:46.
[3] Luke 2:52.

answer the same questions he posed to the teachers in the temple.[1] He was far beyond that now.

Within the cognitive ability of a sinless child, and then of a teenager, and of a young adult, Jesus had come to terms with the fact that profound suffering was his destiny. Doubtless his understanding developed as he began the journey that took him from his baptism in the River Jordan to his baptism in blood on the cross of Calvary. All the while he contemplates, he thinks, he meditates.

But now here in Gethsemane, Jesus is only a few hours away from the full reality of divine judgment. Earlier, Judas had left the upper room, to betray and sell him at a slave's price. Now the Saviour and the remaining eleven apostles have made their way through the streets of Jerusalem and down into the valley. Now they are in the Garden of Gethsemane, and among the olive trees. He stations them – deliberately, don't you think? – some in one location and then, closer to himself, Peter, James and John. They had been together with him to witness the raising of Jairus' daughter, and then up on the Mount of Transfiguration to see his glory. Once again he places them at their station and bids them watch and pray. But Jesus himself goes 'a little farther'.

Now begins this prayer, this intercession. There is nothing quite like it in all Scripture. We see the inner soul of Jesus here, and glimpse something of the deep-seated conflict in which he now seems to be engaged.

It is all too easy to sentimentalize Gethsemane: to focus on the disciples and their inability to stay awake, or to speak about our own 'Gethsemanes', and how we have encountered trials and faced critical decisions. Or we focus on how important it is to 'watch and pray' and the disciples' failure to do so. Yes, for us too 'the spirit is willing but the flesh is weak'. We need to learn how to overcome.

No doubt there are applications we can draw, and lessons we can learn for our own lives. But the focus here is not on the disciples, nor on any lessons that we can learn from them. No. The focus of attention here is Jesus. Here, bowing before his Father, the second person of the Trinity, incarnate, enfleshed, body and soul, he wrestles

[1] Luke 2:46.

with the divine will. If the Mount of Transfiguration pulled aside the veil to reveal his divine glory, it is almost the opposite here. In Gethsemane the veil is pulled aside to reveal his humanity. And the sheer horror of what lies before him now seems to overwhelm him.

There is struggle here. Embattlement is here. Satan is here.

Do you remember how Luke noted that after the wilderness temptations Satan withdrew 'until an opportune time'?[1] He had failed in that first attempt to divert Jesus from the cross. But he had been waiting for a more conducive opportunity. That time had now come. This is it. A cup is being pressed into Jesus' hands. The decision is his – to drink or not to drink? All the factors, all the circumstances, all the contingencies, have now come together. This is the hour of the power of darkness.[2]

We might say, 'All the stars have been aligned.' But the truth is that this is God's sovereign providence. The factors that would bring about the arrest, trial and execution of Jesus are all in place. It is inevitable now. Judas has taken his thirty pieces of silver, selling himself and his soul to the devil. In a short while he will identify him for the soldiers. Jesus knows all this. Yet there remains this last struggle – a struggle in every aspect of his humanity – in his whole being, but particularly in his mind, in his affections, and in his will.

Mind

The conflict begins in Jesus' mind. Think about this for a minute.

'The Son of Man goes as it has been determined', he had said.[3] All the prophecies of Scripture, the ones that he had learned by heart, and in which he had identified himself, his ministry and his destiny – these he had devoted himself to fulfilling. At the last supper he had spoken of the cup of the new covenant symbolizing his blood poured out for many. It was an allusion to the fourth of Isaiah's Songs of the Servant, with its reference to his suffering and death for others. He had already told his disciples that Zechariah 13:7 was about to come true: 'I will strike the shepherd, and the sheep of the flock will be scattered.'[4]

---

[1] Luke 4:13.
[2] Luke 22:53.
[3] Luke 22:22.
[4] Matthew 26:31.

These were Old Testament passages he had learned. He had long meditated on them. He had known what they meant. But now they were rushing together into his mind. Now he was experiencing them.

There is much that is mysterious about Jesus' knowledge of his own identity. The New Testament is largely silent about how he came to understand it. But one day, no doubt, Jesus' mother Mary must have told him about the supernatural manner of his conception and the events that surrounded his birth.[1] Certainly we should not imagine that somehow Jesus 'plugged in' to receive information from his divine nature in order to inform his human nature. No, that is not how Scripture encourages us to think about him. Rather, he progressed in wisdom and understanding.[2]

Since the moment of his conception the Son of God had both divine and human natures. Here we are thinking of his humanity. And in this human nature he 'learned obedience through what he suffered'.[3] He discovered increasingly what it would mean for him to be the Mediator between a Holy God and sinful humanity. For years he had meditated on the Scriptures that revealed that it was 'necessary that the Christ should suffer … and enter into his glory'.[4] Now at last, in Gethsemane, the full significance of all those passages was surely flooding his mind. He did not know and understand, far less experience this all at once, in one great lump of information as it were. Even now – even as late as the evening of his crucifixion – here in Gethsemane, the full extent of the horror of Calvary was probably not fully known to him. It would be much worse than even the grief he saw in the cup which his Father was giving him to drink.

The growing shadow

You know what it is like – at least a little bit. Something is coming; it is looming on the horizon. Yes, it lies in the future, but you know it's coming inevitably. You think about it; you analyse it; at night time it seems to grow bigger and darker, and you can almost feel it. It is coming nearer. The shadow is growing.

---

[1] It was perhaps from her that Luke first heard the same accounts. Luke 1:5-2:52 comes from within Jesus' family circle.

[2] Luke 2:52 (NIV).

[3] Hebrews 5:8.

[4] Luke 24:26.

And now it is here. And it is much worse than you feared; it is more painful than you ever imagined. From a distance you had thought about it in one way or another. But when it actually comes – well, then you realize that you thought only about what it might be *like*; you could not fully understand what it *is* in actual experience. Things that are future, that we know we have to go through – they flash through our minds, But we can only live in the present; we cannot yet experience the full force of the future.

So it was for the Lord Jesus. He was not always as he is here in Gethsemane – prostrate on the ground, crying out to his heavenly Father. But now the full ferocity of the struggle fills his mind and imagination. The 'hour' he had long known would one day come has arrived. The day has dawned; the time is now. He knows it; he understands it; he feels it. He tastes it.

Affections

The struggle in Gethsemane also touches Jesus' emotions.

The Gospel writers employ graphic language to describe his experience. Matthew speaks of how he 'began to be sorrowful'.[1] He was indeed 'a man of sorrows, and acquainted with grief'.[2]

Mark adds that he 'began to be greatly distressed and troubled'.[3] This is the language Paul uses in Philippians 2:26 to describe the distress of Epaphroditus. J. B. Lightfoot, the famous nineteenth century New Testament scholar, suggests it describes 'the confused, restless, half-distracted state which is produced by physical derangement or mental distress, such as grief and shame and disappointment'.[4] At any rate Jesus was emotionally overborne here in Gethsemane. He speaks about his soul being 'very sorrowful, even to death'.[5] Did its very shadow threaten to overwhelm him? Or was he indicating that death itself would be preferable to what he was beginning to experience? Certainly,

[1] Matthew 26:37.
[2] Isaiah 53:3.
[3] Mark 14:33.
[4] J. B. Lightfoot, *Commentary on Paul's Epistle to the Philippians* (London: MacMillan, 1913), 123.
[5] Mark 14:34.

> None of the ransomed ever knew
> How deep were the waters crossed,
> Nor how dark was the night
> that the Lord passed through,
> Ere He found His sheep that was lost.[1]

It is evidence, is it not, of the reality of his humanity? This is no stoic figure without heart, feelings or emotion. His soul is troubled – and troubled to the point of death. Humanly speaking it is unhinging him. If the veil was pulled aside so that Peter, James and John could catch a glimpse of his glory on the Mount of Transfiguration, now it has been pulled aside to show them his heart in all its human sensitivity. Here we see into Jesus' soul, into his inner being. He was 'in an agony'.[2]

Perhaps Jesus initially took these three further into his life simply because he was closest to them.

Mark tells us in an almost offhand way that Jesus chose the disciples in order that they might be 'with him'.[3] But is part of the meaning of this statement that Jesus valued their human companionship? That is a truly and fully human reality – to want companionship, to want to have friends and brothers. Perhaps these three were his closest friends. John, we know, certainly felt he was someone Jesus loved. But now he wants them to be near. His human nature craves encouragement and fellowship. And yet he knows that he must enter territory where they cannot accompany him. And so he goes 'a little farther'.[4] Even visually he is a man apart; his task cannot be either shared with, or assigned to, any other:

> There was no other good enough
> To pay the price of sin;
> He only could unlock the gate
> Of heaven, and let us in.[5]

---

[1] From the hymn by Elizabeth Clephane (1830–69), 'There were ninety and nine that safely lay.'

[2] Luke 22:44.

[3] Mark 3:14.

[4] Matthew 26:39.

[5] From the hymn of Cecil Frances Alexander (1818–95), 'There is a green hill far away.'

He wants them – needs them – to watch and pray with him, and for both himself and themselves. This is the hour of 'the power of darkness'[1] and Jesus must not fail of his task. Salvation depends on it. Your salvation depends on Jesus fulfilling this role – accepting all the obligations of a covenant mediator, standing between God and man, bearing 'our sins in his body on the tree'.[2]

The powers of darkness and hell would do anything to prevent him accomplishing this. Indeed they had done everything they could – even seeking to mastermind his avoidance of the cross through Simon Peter, and now his destruction through the betrayal of Judas. Was this so that he would die on their timetable, by their will, rather than in his active obedience to his Father's will and timetable?

Surely Satan is here too, lurking somewhere in the shadows of the garden.

Jesus found his three disciples sleeping – 'the spirit indeed is willing, but the flesh is weak'.[3] He is undoubtedly referring in the first instance to them. Their flesh is sinful flesh; they have failed him.

But were these words also true of him? For his spirit is willing; but he too is weak flesh and blood. We watch him now. We see him. And he is afraid. He seems to tremble, to shake. He is on the verge of being 'marred, beyond human semblance'.[4] Surely that had implications at the emotional as well as the physical level? The cross is the undoing of humanity. Jesus stands on the edge of that precipice in which an individual comes apart emotionally. Such is the strain. This is what is involved as he enters into the unique horror of making atonement, of being someone who knew no sin but was made sin for others.[5]

When Moses saw God's glory he trembled with fear. But what Moses saw was God in covenant. What Jesus sees is the unmitigated wrath and anger of God unleashed against covenant-breakers. There is no mercy here. He is contemplating taking the place and undergoing the curse due to 'sinners in the hands of an angry God'.[6]

---

[1] Luke 22:53.
[2] 1 Peter 2:24.
[3] Matthew 26:41.
[4] Isaiah 52:14.
[5] 2 Corinthians 5:21.
[6] The title of probably the most famous sermon ever preached on North American soil, by Jonathan Edwards (1703–58). *The Works of Jonathan Edwards* (1834, reprinted,

Paul says that 'the wrath of God is revealed [present tense] from heaven'.[1] But here and now that wrath is always mitigated. It is never the full equivalent of what sin deserves. But there, in the garden, Jesus is contemplating the full force of that unmitigated, holy wrath. He is facing all that it will mean for a sinless person to identify himself with sin and experience the consequences. It had been one thing for him in his sinlessness to come into the realm of sin, to become incarnate and to be surrounded by sin. But to be *reckoned* sin – to 'be made sin for us, who knew no sin'[2] – surely his revulsion of that must have been total?

And so we see him. Look how he trembles and shudders! In his incarnation God's Son had taken 'a reasonable soul and body'.[3] Does it now come within a hair's breadth of breaking down?

But beyond the agony in his mind and affections there is a third dimension to Jesus' experience here in Gethsemane.

Will

In the seventh century A.D. there was an important debate in the Christian church over whether the incarnate Son of God had one will or two wills. Did he have a will that was an aspect of his divine nature and essential to it and, in addition, a will that was essential to his human nature? Some argued that there was only one will. They were called Monothelites.[4] But the church rejected the view that the incarnate Christ has only 'one will and one principle of action'.

Clearly the will of the Son of God in his divine nature is exactly the same as the will of his Father. There can be only one divine will. So when Jesus speaks about 'my will' and 'your will', the reference in 'my will' is to the will, the volitional activity of his human nature. Notice carefully – and reverently, for it is breathtaking to hear – that as he contemplates what lies before him Jesus says:

> Father, is there not some other way? I see the cross, I understand it now in a way that I could not have done in my human nature before now. But in my mind, in all of my

---

Edinburgh: Banner of Truth Trust, 1974), vol. 2, 7-12.

[1] Romans 1:18.

[2] 2 Corinthians 5:21.

[3] The language is borrowed from *The Confession of Chalcedon*, A.D. 451.

[4] From the Greek words 'one' (*monos*) and 'will' (*thelēma*).

affections as I look down this dark and foreboding tunnel – is there not some other way? I wish there were, for I can hardly bear the thought of experiencing a sense of being God-forsaken!

In his divine mind of course, he knew that there was no other way. He had agreed with the Father in the counsels of eternity that all this would be necessary in order to save sinners, and that he would go through with the agreement. But that information, that perfect knowledge of his future obedience is not something to which his human mind was privy to the same degree earlier in his life.

And so here we witness the Son of God, the second person of the eternal Trinity, praying – yes, in utter and complete submission to his heavenly Father – pleading, beseeching, agonizing, crying to his Father in weakness and vulnerability: 'Let this cup pass from me … nevertheless …'

This is Jesus, as we have never seen him before; not like this. Nor shall we ever see him again in this manner.

There are two seeming causes for his distress. The first is the nature of 'the hour'.[1]

The hour

Throughout his earlier ministry Jesus' watchword was 'The hour is not yet come.'[2] This was why he told his disciples to maintain a certain silence about his messianic identity, doubtless in case he was mistaken for a politically-driven messiah – an aspiration already present in the culture of Jesus' day. The 'hour' when the true nature of his messiahship would be revealed was 'not yet'.

Then, after Caesarea Philippi, it becomes clear that he was heading directly towards this 'hour' as he set a course that would eventually lead to Jerusalem and the cross. It was as if a door had turned on its hinges following Simon Peter's confession.

But now, here in Gethsemane, this 'hour' is not something future. It is not even impending but still to arrive. It has come; it is here; it is now. Now the unmitigated wrath of God is rapidly coming over the

---

[1] See Luke 22:53 and John 17:1. For other references to this 'hour' see Matthew 26:45; Mark 14:35, 41; Luke 22:53; John 2:4; 7:30; 8:20; 12:23, 27; 13:1; 16:32; 17:1.

[2] Cf. his words to his mother recorded in John 2:4.

horizon. And so, perhaps remembering the cup of blessing he had left on the table in the upper room, and conscious of all that the prophets had said and written about the cup of the wrath of God,[1] he prays: 'My Father, if it be possible, let this cup pass from me.'[2]

Jesus is making this request to the Father who loves him, who always hears him,[3] and who has never refused him. What a sublime mystery there is here as the second person of the Godhead, incarnate in our weak flesh (although without sin), expresses a resolve to do the Father's will. Every holy emotion in him must have shrunk from drinking the cup. His 'obedience to the point of death, even the death of the cross' did not come without him being in an 'agony'.[4]

Sometimes people tell us that the epitome of Christian discipleship and maturity is that we *instantaneously* yield to whatever it is that God is asking us to do. After all, if we are *really* spiritual should not that resolve come easily? But it did not come that way for Jesus.[5] It was not instantaneous for him. It was hard, and sore. But that means that there was something all the more sublime about his submission to his Father's will and his willingness to die the death of the cross as the means of our salvation.

And so he cries, 'Father, if it is possible, let this cup pass from me.'

'*If* it is possible.' His human mind, not privy to omniscience, to all knowledge, probes the divine mind and will: 'Father, is there some knowledge here, is there some information that I am missing here, that perhaps makes possible a different route for us to take?'

Do we shudder at the thought of Jesus saying this? So we should. For we are on the brink here, on the edge of a precipice. Our salvation hangs in the balance here. Were Satan's hopes momentarily raised here at the thought that, perhaps, now at last he had caught the Saviour wavering from the Father's will?

Father, if it is possible …

Do you see what this means? Almost inevitably we hesitate to say

---

[1] See, for example, Isaiah 51:17, 22; Jeremiah 25:15, 17; Ezekiel 23:31-33; Habakkuk 2:16.

[2] Matthew 26:39.

[3] John 11:42.

[4] Philippians 2:8; Luke 22:44.

[5] Nor for the apostle Paul. See 2 Corinthians 12:8.

it. For he is saying, 'I don't want to go down this road.' His holy humanity cries out 'not this road – not the darkness in which I will be left crying, "My God, I am forsaken! Why?"'

Jesus is rightly afraid. 'No man feared death like this man', said Luther.[1] The Saviour trembles. This is sorrow unto death. It feels as though it could destroy him. 'His sweat', Luke tells us, 'became like great drops of blood falling down to the ground'[2] – and that was *after* an angel had come to strengthen him. So let us not think that because he is the Son of God the trial that Jesus is going through is any less severe, the burden any lighter. This is a struggle to the very limits, even although he is upheld by the Spirit and strengthened by an angel. This is a moment of trial, a moment of temptation, a moment of testing that surpasses anything that has taken place since the beginning of creation. No wonder then that Alexander Whyte once remarked that next to the Lord Jesus himself he wished that his first conversation in heaven might be with the angel who came to strengthen him.

The obedience

But then there comes submission: 'Not my will, Father – not even the pure undefiled will of my human nature that has never entertained sin – but your will be done.'

The New Testament describes the work of Jesus on our behalf in several different ways. But central to them all is his obedience.

No voice except that of Jesus can be heard in Gethsemane. Yet surely his Father was thinking, 'Son, – know that I love you. I have always loved you, and always will.' Perhaps we can imagine him quietly singing,

> My Jesus, I love Thee, I know Thou art mine ...
> If ever I loved Thee, my Jesus, 'tis now.[3]

But no voice is heard here. Yet the word of God that he had rightly understood, and in relationship to which he had resisted the devil's temptations, now proved altogether reliable. Psalm 91 – whose false

---

[1] Cited in C. E. B. Cranfield, *The Gospel According to St. Mark: A Commentary* (Cambridge: Cambridge University Press, 1959), 431.

[2] Luke 22:44.

[3] From the hymn by William Featherstone (1846–73), 'My Jesus, I love Thee, I know Thou art mine.' Featherstone apparently wrote this hymn in his teenage years.

and satanic interpretation he had refused on the pinnacle of the Jerusalem temple – was wonderfully true now: 'He will command his angels concerning you … on their hands they will bear you up … the serpent you will trample underfoot.'[1]

So the last Adam, unlike the first Adam, obeys. He yields. He enters into the darkness where no voice is heard repeating the words of the River and the Mountain, 'This is my beloved Son, with whom I am well pleased.'[2] But he trusts and he obeys. Had he not himself confessed more than once that he had come not to do his own will but the will of the Father who had sent him?[3]

The same disciples who had slept on the Mount of Transfiguration were sleeping again in the Garden of Gethsemane. We dare not be too hard on them. It is dark. They are attempting to keep watch in the dead of night. And there is now an intensity of emotion that makes them even more tired – a tiredness from the kind of stress that exhausts. Yes, they fail. Truly the flesh is weak. But all this simply highlights Jesus, our glorious Saviour. There is none like him. He is awake; he obeys; he yields to the will of his heavenly Father. And in this we see once again the veil being pulled aside to give us a glimpse of his obedience – all in the context of his sorrow, his soul-trouble, his overwhelming sense of heaviness.

What a sight this is to behold! The Saviour says, 'See, the hour is at hand, and the Son of Man is betrayed into the hands of sinners. Rise, let us be going; see, my betrayer is at hand.'[4]

There is something of a military tone in Jesus' words here.[5] All of his preliminary training is now complete. He has passed every test and now he takes his place for the final battle, resolved, determined, submissive and yielding to his heavenly Father's will. Now let the final battle commence! Soon the serpent will be trampled underfoot, according to the ancient promises.[6]

---

[1] Psalm 91:11-13. Luke records the ministry of such an angel, Luke 22:43.

[2] Matthew 3:17 and 17:5.

[3] John 5:30; 6:38.

[4] Matthew 26:45-46.

[5] As, it has been argued, in John 14:31 which is also set in the context of conflict with Satan as 'the ruler of this world'.

[6] Genesis 3:15; Psalm 91:13; Isaiah 65:25c.

Jesus now marches towards the final conflict. Yes, there will be soldiers with swords, and religious leaders with murder in their hearts and on their tongues, and an earthly king from the Herodian family that has so hated the prophets of God. And, yes, there is the power of the Roman Empire under whose governor Pontius Pilate he will be falsely condemned to death and executed. But behind and beneath all such earthly powers he is entering the lists against 'our ancient foe', going into battle against Satan to spoil principalities and powers and make a show of them, triumphing over them in the cross.[1] As Luther has taught us to sing,

> For us fights the Proper Man
> And He must win the battle.

This is Jesus in Gethsemane.
Now only the cross awaits him.

No incident in the life of the Saviour gives us quite such a glimpse of who he really was, or the immensity of the task that he was called to accomplish for us, or the depth of what he became for us, or how deeply he loves us.

Indeed,

> There was no other good enough
> To pay the price of sin.
> He only could unlock the gate
> Of heaven and let us in.

[1] Cf. Colossians 2:15.

6. The Cross – *Passion*

Who is He, on yonder tree,
Dies in grief and agony?

> *'Tis the Lord! O wondrous story!*
> *'Tis the Lord! the King of glory!*
> *At His feet we humbly fall;*
> *Crown Him, Crown Him Lord of all.*

Mark 15:1-39

And as soon as it was morning, the chief priests held a consultation with the elders and scribes and the whole Council. And they bound Jesus and led him away and delivered him over to Pilate. ² And Pilate asked him, 'Are you the King of the Jews?' And he answered him, 'You have said so.' ³ And the chief priests accused him of many things. ⁴ And Pilate again asked him, 'Have you no answer to make? See how many charges they bring against you.' ⁵ But Jesus made no further answer, so that Pilate was amazed. ⁶ Now at the feast he used to release for them one prisoner for whom they asked. ⁷ And among the rebels in prison, who had committed murder in the insurrection, there was a man called Barabbas. ⁸ And the crowd came up and began to ask Pilate to do as he usually did for them. ⁹ And he answered them, saying, 'Do you want me to release for you the King of the Jews?' ¹⁰ For he perceived that it was out of envy that the chief priests had delivered him up. ¹¹ But the chief priests stirred up the crowd to have him release for them Barabbas instead. ¹² And Pilate again said to them, 'Then what shall I do with the man you call the King of the Jews?' ¹³ And they cried out again, 'Crucify him.' ¹⁴ And Pilate said to them, 'Why, what evil has he done?' But they shouted all the more, 'Crucify him.' ¹⁵ So Pilate, wishing to satisfy the crowd, released for them Barabbas, and having scourged Jesus, he delivered him to be crucified. ¹⁶ And the soldiers led him away inside the palace (that is, the governor's headquarters), and they called together the whole battalion. ¹⁷ And they clothed him in a purple cloak, and twisting together a crown of thorns, they put it on him. ¹⁸ And they began to salute him, 'Hail, King of the Jews!' ¹⁹ And they were striking his head with a reed and spitting on him and kneeling down in homage to him. ²⁰ And when they had mocked him, they stripped him of the purple cloak and put his own clothes on him. And they led him out to crucify him. ²¹ And they compelled a passerby, Simon of Cyrene, who was coming in from the country, the father of Alexander and Rufus, to carry his cross. ²² And they brought him to the place called Golgotha (which means Place of a Skull). ²³ And they offered him wine mixed with myrrh, but he did not take it. ²⁴ And they crucified him and divided his garments among them, casting lots for them, to decide what each should take. ²⁵ And it was the third hour when they crucified him. ²⁶ And the inscription of the charge against him read, 'The King of the Jews.' ²⁷ And with him they crucified two robbers, one on his right and one on his left. ²⁹ And those who passed by derided him, wagging their heads and saying, 'Aha! You who would destroy the temple and rebuild it in three days, ³⁰ save yourself, and come down from the cross!' ³¹ So also the chief priests with the scribes mocked him to one another, saying, 'He saved others; he cannot save himself. ³² Let the Christ, the King of Israel, come down now from the cross that we may see and believe.' Those who were crucified with him also reviled him. ³³ And when the sixth hour had come, there was darkness over the whole land until the ninth hour. ³⁴ And at the ninth hour Jesus cried with a loud voice, 'Eloi, Eloi, lema sabachthani?' which means, 'My God, my God, why have you forsaken me?' ³⁵ And some of the bystanders hearing it said, 'Behold, he is calling Elijah.' ³⁶ And someone ran and filled a sponge with sour wine, put it on a reed and gave it to him to drink, saying, 'Wait, let us see whether Elijah will come to take him down.' ³⁷ And Jesus uttered a loud cry and breathed his last. ³⁸ And the curtain of the temple was torn in two, from top to bottom. ³⁹ And when the centurion, who stood facing him, saw that in this way he breathed his last, he said, 'Truly this man was the Son of God!'

OUR last glimpse of Jesus was of him rising from his prostrate position in Gethsemane, wakening his disciples, and readying them for the nightmare to come.

The 'hour' has arrived. The power of darkness descends on the garden. Now 'Judas, having procured a band of soldiers, and some officers from the chief priests and the Pharisees went there with lanterns and torches and weapons.'[1] Jesus had earlier mentioned Zechariah's prophecy: 'I will strike the shepherd, and the sheep will be scattered.'[2] Now it is fulfilled. He is arrested and the disciples flee, including (as Mark notes, perhaps like an artist painting himself into his own work) a young man who, struggling to escape his pursuers, did so only by the narrowest of margins.[3]

Trial after trial

A series of trials now begins.

First of all Jesus is brought before the High Priest. In the dead of night a 'grand jury' of chief priests, elders and scribes illegally gathers.[4] He faces a prejudiced and corrupt court who will act as prosecution counsel, jury, and judge, and for good measure false witnesses. Asked directly if he was the Christ, Jesus once again identified himself as 'the Son of Man' who would fulfil the vision recorded in Daniel chapter 7. One day he would be seated at the right hand of God and seen coming in clouds of glory.[5]

Meanwhile, as though in a parallel universe, Simon Peter can be

[1] John 18:3.

[2] Mark 14:27. Cf. Zechariah 13:7.

[3] Mark 14:51-2: 'They seized him, but he left the linen cloth [which was all he was wearing] and ran away naked.'

[4] It was contrary both to law and to natural justice for a person to be thus tried at night.

[5] See Daniel 7:9-28. 'Son of Man' is Jesus' chosen way of describing himself.

spotted in the courtyard of the High Priest's residence. By the fire where he is warming himself he denies ever knowing his Master – once, twice, and finally, in a state of sheer panic with a self-maledictory curse, a third time!

And then – as John Mark records the story which early church tradition suggests is actually Simon Peter's own account – these parallel worlds come together. A rooster that might have been heard earlier crowing in the background now crows a second time. Peter remembers the prophecy of Jesus, 'Before the rooster crows twice, you will deny me three times.'[1] Broken in soul, he hurries out into the darkness of the streets of Jerusalem and weeps bitter tears of repentance.

Did John Mark deliberately spare his mentor the further detail that Luke painted into his narrative? 'The Lord turned and looked at Peter. And Peter remembered the saying of the Lord ...'[2] Or was Peter so deeply ashamed that he could never bring himself publicly to share that part of the darkest night of his soul, having no words to describe that look in the eyes of the Saviour?

As soon as dawn broke, the chief priests held further talks with their advisers, along with the entire Sanhedrin (the Jewish ruling body). Having been spat upon, blindfolded, and physically abused, and made the butt of cynical mocking ('Prophesy! Tell us who hit you!'), Jesus was now bound, and handed over to the Roman governor – with a plan in place to make sure that Pilate would be forced to execute him.

There is a remarkable dignity and restraint in the way the Gospel writers record the events of Jesus' final hours. It is expressed in both the words and the music of the greatest hymns written on the theme of the crucifixion. That is certainly true of Paul Gerhardt's 'O Sacred Head sore wounded' set so movingly to J. S. Bach's arrangement of the *Passion Chorale*:

> O Sacred head, sore wounded,
>   With grief and shame bowed down,
> How scornfully surrounded
>   With thorns, Thine only crown!

[1] Mark 14:72. Cf. 14:30-31.
[2] Luke 22:61. The 'word of the Lord' refers undoubtedly to Luke 22:31-32.

What language shall I borrow
To thank Thee, dearest Friend,
For this Thy dying sorrow,
Thy pity without end?
O make me Thine for ever;
And should I fainting be,
Lord, let me never, never,
Outlive my love to Thee![1]

The same slow dignity echoes through

When I survey the wondrous cross
On which the Prince of Glory died,
My richest gain I count but loss,
And pour contempt on all my pride.[2]

But (perhaps to our surprise) it is to other hymns that we need to look if we are to get to the heart of the message the Gospel writers have woven into their narrative of our Lord's passion. Both Paul Gerhardt and Isaac Watts touch deep emotions and describe true and important responses to their descriptions of the Saviour's love. But the key to Calvary is not that it evokes a response of profound emotions, or even that the love displayed there 'Demands my soul, my life, my all.'[3] No. It is not so much how Jesus' death touches us deeply but what he accomplished in that death that is central to the gospel.

That is what is so well captured in a hymn written originally for children:

There is a green hill far away,
Without[4] a city wall,
Where the dear Lord was crucified,
Who died to save us all.

We may not know, we cannot tell
What pains He had to bear;
But we believe it was for us
He hung and suffered there.

[1] Written by Paul Gerhardt (1607–76) and translated by J. W. Alexander (1804–59).
[2] By Isaac Watts (1674–1748).
[3] As in the closing line of 'When I survey the wondrous cross.'
[4] That is, 'outside'.

There was no other good enough
To pay the price of sin;
He only could unlock the gate
Of heaven, and let us in.[1]

The same message is expressed even more boldly by Philip Bliss:

Man of Sorrows! Wondrous name
For the Son of God, who came
Ruined sinners to reclaim!
Hallelujah! what a Saviour!

Bearing shame and scoffing rude,
In my place condemned He stood;
Sealed my pardon with His blood:
Hallelujah! what a Saviour!

Guilty, vile, and helpless we;
Spotless Lamb of God was He:
Full atonement, – can it be?
Hallelujah! What a Saviour![2]

During the twentieth century, that particular hymn began to be carefully omitted from the worship of many churches. People did not object to being moved *emotionally* by the thought of Jesus' death; but they no longer appreciated describing themselves *biblically* as 'ruined sinners' or confessing themselves to be 'guilty, vile and helpless'. But remove this perspective on the cross and we tear the heart and soul out of the Christian gospel.

It is not stretching the imagination too far to assume that Philip Bliss had just been meditating on the fourteenth and fifteenth chapters of Mark's Gospel when he penned these words. His hymn seems to follow the core experiences described there:

Bearing shame and scoffing rude,
In my place condemned He stood;
Sealed my pardon with His blood …

Certainly we can say there is something spiritually amiss in us if at the end of reading these verses we do not bow down before the throne

[1] Written by Cecil Frances Alexander (1818–95).
[2] Written by Philip P. Bliss (1838–76).

of God and say

Hallelujah! what a Saviour!

'Bearing shame and scoffing rude'

From the moment of his betrayal by Judas and subsequent arrest, until his body was hanging limp in death on the cross, Jesus was deliberately and persistently put to shame.

There can be few more shameful ways of betrayal than by a kiss. It was but the harbinger of what was to come.

The great Roman orator Cicero commented in a famous speech before the Roman Senate that 'the very mention of the cross should be far removed not only from a Roman citizen's body, but from his mind, his eyes, his ears'.[1] It was a systematic way of shaming and exposing a person in public.

The author of the Letter (perhaps better the 'Sermon') to the Hebrews states explicitly that Jesus experienced this 'shame'.[2] In fact for as many as twenty hours the Lord Jesus was subjected to unmitigated, relentless and ruthless shame, climaxing in the final exposure of the cross.

The well-known words of Hebrews 12:1-2 urge us to 'fix our eyes on Jesus who for the joy that was set before him endured the cross, despising the shame'.[3] But it would be a mistake if we were to breathe a sigh of relief, thinking, 'Thank God he despised the shame! Thank God for the joy! That is a relief to me. I can hardly bear to think that he experienced it.' But that is virtually the very reverse of what these words mean. The shame was unbearable. It was only the intensity of the joy of the glory beyond it that enabled him to despise it.

So we must never forget the *shame of the cross*. It is written all over the narrative of our Saviour's passion.

[1] Cicero (in a speech given sometime in the mid-fifties B.C.) *Pro Rabirio Postumo*, V. 16.

[2] Hebrews 12:2. The author also hints that the only way to deal with such imposed shame is to 'despise' it. To do so a person must necessarily have his or her gaze fixed on the greater end and purpose for which he or she is willing to experience it.

[3] Hebrews 12:2 (NIV).

The crucifixion was in the deepest sense a liturgy of shame; but it was also a fulfilment of the Scriptures.

The Gospel writers tell their story through words informed by an understanding of what God the Father was actually accomplishing through Jesus' death. He is the obedient Servant of the Lord. He fulfils the prophecy that he would suffer by being oppressed and afflicted, by being led as a lamb to the slaughter, and being dumb like a sheep before her shearers, not opening his mouth.[1]

In the midst of this onslaught of shame the Lord Jesus speaks few words. He absorbs into himself the shame he does not merit as he is taken from one shaming occasion to another. He is led to the High Priest and there shamed by religious leaders. Attempts are made to destroy his reputation for integrity by false witnesses. Jesus is silent in the face of all charges. He does not protest, 'These are lies.' He absorbs the shame as though he was himself the liar and falsifier.

And then, as Jesus is condemned by the religious leaders, they deliberately add to his shame: 'some began to spit on him and to cover his face and to strike him, saying to him "Prophesy!"'[2]

In this condition, Jesus is bound and taken to Pontius Pilate.[3] Alas for poor, weak, pressured Pontius Pilate. He is no match for these religious grandmasters who will manoeuvre him into defeat in the chess game they have so carefully planned. He hopes for an escape route in the Passover custom of setting free a prisoner as an act of clemency and good will towards the Jewish people. But he badly miscalculates. He washes his hands (literally) of the whole affair, releases Barabbas ('son of a father') and exchanges him for the Son of the heavenly Father.

What happened next to Jesus?

He was scourged.[4] The was done with a whip-like instrument that had shells, or pieces of bone or metal embedded into the ends of long

[1] Isaiah 53:7.

[2] Mark 14:65. In this macabre game of 'Blind Man's Buff' the spiritually blind taunt the physically blinded Jesus and mock him by demanding if he can 'see' who hit him (one of the Hebrew words for a prophet is ro´ēh, a 'seer').

[3] Mark 15:1.

[4] Mark 15:15.

thongs of leather.[1] Its function was humiliation and weakening. So violent was the scourging that it sometimes killed men before their crucifixion could take place. Perhaps soldiers gritted their teeth and regarded it as a severe mercy, preferable to the long hours of death by slow asphyxiation on the cross.

Mark tells us that as Jesus was handed over to the Roman soldiers for crucifixion, they took him inside the headquarters. Far from the prying eyes of his own people, these members of the most disciplined military force in the first century surrounded and exposed Jesus further.

We rarely pause to contemplate this scene.

Mark tells us 'they called together the whole battalion'. One or more of their leaders has decided that this is an opportunity for the whole barracks to be entertained. A battalion, or cohort, consisted usually of somewhere between two hundred and six hundred men. Some, doubtless, were on duty. But every available man is invited to come and watch the shaming of Jesus of Nazareth. There he stands, clothed in the purple garb of the kingship they mock, wearing a crown of thorns: 'Hail, King of the Jews!' More – they strike him with a reed, spit on him, and then with cruel cynicism, kneel before him.

The 'fun' is soon over. They strip him of the purple robe. Now it becomes clear they had first stripped him of his own clothes. Mark's Gospel gently lets his readers know the terrible truth. They had *stripped* him. They would almost certainly do so again at Golgotha. This was, in essence, a form of mass gang rape. *Ecce homo* indeed. Behold the man, now dehumanized by man, that we who have been unmanned in sin might become truly human again.

So now the one who was 'gentle and lowly in heart', who offered to the bruised and beaten 'rest' for their souls[2] is treated roughly, with arrogance, and is himself bruised and beaten down.

This was the dreaded wine he had seen in the cup his Father pressed into his hands in the Garden of Gethsemane.

It must have seemed as if, ever so slowly, Psalm 23 was beginning to run in reverse gear. Jesus now lacked everything; there was nowhere for his soul to graze; soon, in the valley of the shadow of death evil would

---

[1] Mark 15:15. Unusually for a Bible translation, the ESV includes an explanatory footnote here.

[2] Matthew 11:29.

seem to reign; there would be no comfort for him in God. Yes, a table would be spread in the presence of his enemies, but the only object on it would be this cup of dereliction and distress. Religious men's spittle anointed his head; no goodness, no mercy is shown here. In utter alone-ness he would soon feel cast out from the house of the Lord.

And yet in that wine there gazed back at him a reflection. He saw it now, far more clearly than the prophet Isaiah had done – although he had 'searched and enquired carefully, inquiring what person or time the Spirit of Christ ... was indicating when he predicted the sufferings of Christ'.[1]

Did Jesus catch any glimpse in the wine cup from which he was drinking or any reflection of 'the subsequent glories'?[2] If he was indeed the Servant prophesied in Isaiah, as he had long known and believed, then the Scriptures gave him hope; for the joy set before him he would endure the shame.

But the joy and the glory follow the shame. They cannot precede it:

> The Lord GOD has opened my ear,
>   and I was not rebellious;
>   I turned not backward.
> I gave my back to those who strike,
>   and my cheeks to those who pull out the beard;
> I hid not my face
>   from disgrace and spitting.[3]

Isaiah had heard the Lord say,

> Behold, my servant shall act wisely;
>   he shall be high and lifted up,
>   and shall be exalted.[4]

But first a dreadful antithesis. So dreadful that Isaiah seems instinctively to address the Servant himself:

> As many were astonished at *you* –

And then returning to his accustomed descriptive language:

---

[1] 1 Peter 1:10-11.
[2] 1 Peter 1:11.
[3] Isaiah 50:5-6.
[4] Isaiah 52:13.

His appearance was so marred, beyond human
   semblance,
and his form beyond that of the children of
   mankind.[1]

Yes, the Servant will be exalted. One day kings will close their mouths in his presence. But the marring must come before the majesty – a marring 'beyond human semblance'. As J. Alec Motyer poignantly notes, the dereliction is so extensive that it raises the question, 'Is he still human?'[2] His sufferings at the hands of men are intended to un-man the Lord Jesus, to demean and shame his humanity – this holy, innocent, gracious Saviour who had gone about doing good.

There is outer darkness and inner darkness here.

The last journey

Now the last journey begins. The cross beam on which he will soon be stretched is placed over his shoulders. He must carry it to Calvary himself.

But then comes a moment of light in the darkness. Simon of Cyrene (a Libyan, presumably) is coming into the city from the country and is conscripted to carry Jesus' cross beam to Golgotha.

The 'footnote' Mark appends to Simon's name: he was 'the father of Alexander and Rufus',[3] presses a pause button in the narrative. His words can mean only one thing: these two men were known to John Mark and almost certainly to his first readers. Into this dark tapestry Mark weaves a single coloured thread. Even from the *Via Dolorosa* there was a path that he hints led to faith in Christ for this man's sons (and for himself too, and perhaps their mother?[4]).

Then, at last Jesus arrives at the hill of shame, Golgotha – a sight chosen in order to maximize the impact of the event by giving passers-by an opportunity to increase the shame, as indeed they did.[5]

The crucifixion squad offered Jesus the customary analgesic of wine mixed with myrrh, which he declined. Once more he is stripped,

[1] Isaiah 52:14.

[2] J. Alec Motyer, *The Prophecy of Isaiah* (Leicester: Inter-Varsity Press, 1993), 425.

[3] Mark 15:21.

[4] Is the Rufus of Romans 16:13 the Rufus of Mark 15:21? If so it seems the entire family became disciples.

[5] See Mark 15:29.

and the executioners get on with their cruel work. Three Greek words describe the darkest moment in human history: *kai staurousin auton* – 'and they crucified him'. Mark will say no more. His camera slowly descends from its focus on Jesus to the scene at the foot of the cross: soldiers throwing dice to see who will win his garments. Does he also die naked, as seems to have been the norm in crucifixions? Then indeed he is the Second Man, the Last Adam, without clothing to hide him from the shame of the cross. Now the last vestiges of the common grace of life have been torn away from him. No one sees yet what the Gospel writers would later see: he is unclothed to bear our sin that we might be clothed with his righteousness.

And then the mocking begins all over again. In the presence of the crucified Lord Jesus ordinary people become animals. And with them the chief priests and the scribes – the bishops, archbishops, and moderators of religious assemblies of the day – the religious leaders are mocking him in their unmitigated sense of triumph. They catcall at him. Even those who were crucified with him mock him.[1]

Now Psalm 22 has come full circle:

> I am a worm and not a man,
>   scorned by mankind and despised by the people.
> All who see me mock me;
>   they make mouths at me; they wag their heads;
> 'He trusts in the Lord; let him deliver him;
>   let him rescue him, for he delights in him!'
>
> Many bulls encompass me;
>   strong bulls of Bashan surround me;
> they open wide their mouths at me,
>   like a ravening and roaring lion.
>
> I am poured out like water,
>   and all my bones are out of joint;
> my heart is like wax;
>   it is melted within my breast;
> my strength is dried up like a potsherd,
>   and my tongue sticks to my jaws;
>   you lay me in the dust of death.

[1] Mark does not pause in his rapidly moving description of events to tell us that one of these men turned to Christ in faith. See Luke 23:39-43.

> For dogs encompass me;
>> a company of evildoers encircles me;
> They have pierced my hands and feet –
>> I can count all my bones –
> they stare and gloat over me;
> they divide my garments among them,
>> and for my clothing they cast lots.[1]

Darkness falls unexpectedly. This is the darkness of the as yet unformed creation, the darkness of Abraham's dream, and the darkness of Egypt's night when the angel of death visited the land and the firstborn died.[2] It is also the darkness of the cloud of God's presence. And in that darkness, in Christ, God fulfils his self-maledictory oath to Abraham to bring blessing even if it should cost him his only Son.

Jesus cries out to God in an impenetrable sense of God-forsakenness: *'Eloi, Eloi, lema sabachthani?'* But he is not crying for Elijah as some mishear and who see in his cry a final opportunity to mock him – 'Let's fetch him a drink and make him last a little longer, and let's see if Elijah will come to rescue him.'

Yes, Elijah was to return before the Day of the Lord. But he had already come in John the Baptist. They had not recognized the fulfilment of prophecy.[3] They had ignored the final warning. Their refusal to repent was clear for all to see. All that was left now was the promised Day of the Lord.

If we stand back from the details we have examined and look at Mark's canvas as a whole, we can hardly fail to notice that there is a triple mocking here, a three-fold shame.

• Jesus is being mocked as prophet – he said he would rebuild the temple in three days; what of his prophecy now?

• He is being mocked as priest – he said he would save others, but he cannot save himself.

• And he is being mocked as king – let him show his power and come down from the cross!

---

[1] Psalm 22:6-8, 12-18.
[2] See Genesis 1:2; 15:1-21; Exodus 10:21-29.
[3] See Malachi 4:5 and Mark 9:12-13.

In all three of his offices as our Mediator he is

Bearing shame and scoffing rude.

But there is more.

'In my place condemned He stood'

The Gospels describe a life lived in real space-time history. But we should never read them as though they were merely historical narratives or straightforward biographies telling us facts about a significant life. The word 'Gospel' – good news – should give us a clue. In some ways these books are more like sermons than biographies. You do not take thirty to forty per cent of the pages of a biography in order to chronicle the events of the last week of the subject's life, or fifteen per cent of it to describe his last twenty-four hours. No, in these pages there is a message woven into the very texture of the story. We find it embedded in the narrative.

It is always impressive to watch an art specialist standing in front of a great work in order to explain its significance. The work is not merely paint on canvas, or even beauty, to the expert interpreter. He understands the wordless language of art – the background story, the symbolism, how the painting reflects the history of art and the context in which it was composed. He can even tell us when one great artist is 'quoting' another.

Something similar is true of the Gospels. Woven into the way the story is told is the *meaning* of the story, the *message* of the gospel itself.

The meaning is this. Jesus is on trial before the highest court of the purest religion in the world. But it has been corrupted by sin. Although demonstrably innocent, he is condemned. He is also on trial before the most sophisticated justice system in antiquity. Again, although demonstrably innocent, he is condemned.

Not only is this obviously the case. Again and again the narrative specifically underlines that the very people who condemn Jesus as guilty recognize and acknowledge that he is in fact innocent.

This paradox becomes even more intriguing – and yet enlightening – when we see the two basic charges which were brought against Jesus, for both of which he is condemned.

The first is *the religious charge* that he has committed blasphemy and therefore deserves to die, under the condemnation of God.

The second is *the civil charge* that he has committed treason against Caesar by making himself a king and therefore deserves to die, under the condemnation of the Roman Empire.

It sometimes happens that a man may be falsely charged in a human court and found guilty. But his accusers do not acknowledge his innocence. Rather they argue vigorously, if deceitfully and maliciously, for his guilt. But in the case of Jesus, all four Gospel writers bring out the way in which he was acknowledged as innocent *by his accusers* but was nevertheless condemned as guilty.

Jesus is not guilty of the religious court's charge of blasphemy. Apart from any other consideration the false witnesses to his blasphemy cannot agree. He is being condemned for a crime of which he is innocent.

Nor is he guilty of the civil court's charge of treason. He had, after all, said, 'Render to Caesar the things that are Caesar's, and to God the things that are God's.'[1] Pilate himself makes clear: 'I find nothing worthy of death in this man.' How then can he say, 'I will scourge and have him crucified'?

Do you notice the real plot line of the narrative? Miss this and we miss the whole point of the Gospels. What is really happening here?

• Jesus has been charged with blasphemy of which he is innocent, but is found guilty and crucified.

• He has been charged with treason of which he is innocent, but is found guilty and crucified.

Virtually everyone in the cast of this divine drama is constrained to proclaim the innocence of Jesus. The whole story is crying out to us:

> Why, then, when he is innocent is he crucified?
> Why, when he is guilt-free, is he treated as guilty?

Philip Bliss knew the answer:

> In my place condemned He stood
> Sealed my pardon with His blood.

[1] Matthew 22:21.

'In my place'

Christians throughout the ages have understood the mystery here. These two charges of blasphemy and treason are actually the charges of which we are all guilty before the judgment seat of God. These are the crimes against our names on the charge sheet of heaven.

We are guilty of blasphemy in that we have made ourselves, rather than God, the centre of our universe. We have dethroned him and enthroned ourselves. At best we have seen him as our servant, there to be whatever we want him to be, as we foolishly say, 'The way I like to think about God is …' Blasphemy! It is no small thing to create our own god in our own likeness.

And then there is the charge of treason. We have rebelled against his authority over us. We have said insistently, even if subtly, 'It will be my will that will be done on earth. And I anticipate that I will get my way in heaven too.' And so we are as guilty of the second charge of treason as we are of the first charge of blasphemy.

This is the 'back story' to the Passion narrative. Everything about it says to us: 'Jesus is not dying for his own sins. He has none.' But if he is not being crucified for his own sins, why then is he being crucified? The answer is obvious, isn't it? It is certainly made obvious in the pages of the New Testament: *He is being crucified for us.* This is the consistent explanation of the New Testament:

> God did not spare his own Son but gave him up *for us all.*

> He who knew no sin was made sin *for us* that we might become in him the righteousness of God.

> The Son of God loved me, and gave himself *for me.*

> He was made a curse *for us* that all the blessings of God's grace might flow into our lives.[1]

Jesus took my place. He died for my sins. This was what Isaiah had seen. He did not know how it was going to happen. Nor did he know when the Lord Jesus would come or even precisely who he would be. But he knew that the coming Saviour would be led as a lamb to the slaughter, and be dumb like a sheep standing before its shearers. He would be wounded for our transgressions, and crushed for our iniquities; he would bear the chastisement that would bring us peace; and

---

[1] See Romans 8:32; 2 Corinthians 5:21; Galatians 2:20; 3:13.

with the beatings he would receive we would be made whole. The Lord would cause all our iniquities to meet on him, our sin-bearer.[1]

This is why Jesus remained so silent. His was not the silence of guilt and shame as ours is,[2] but the silence of willingness to accept these charges instead of me: 'In my place condemned he stood.'

The hymn writer Christopher Idle has captured this well:

> He stood before the court
> on trial instead of us;
> he met its power to hurt,
> condemned to face the cross:
> our king, accused
> of treachery;
> our God, accused
> of blasphemy!
>
> These are the crimes that tell
> the tale of human guilt;
> our sins, our death, our hell
> on these the case is built:
> to this world's powers
> their Lord stays dumb;
> the guilt is ours,
> no answers come.
>
> The sentence must be passed,
> the unknown prisoner killed;
> the price is paid at last,
> the law of God fulfilled:
> he takes our blame,
> and from that day
> the accuser's claim
> is wiped away.
>
> Shall we be judged and tried?
> In Christ our trial is done;
> we live, for he has died,
> our condemnation gone:
> in Christ are we
> both dead and raised,
> alive and free
> his name be praised!

[1] Isaiah 53:5-6.
[2] See Romans 3:19-20.

So his crucifixion meant 'bearing shame and scoffing rude'. It meant 'in my place condemned he stood'.

But it also meant that he –

'Sealed my pardon with His blood'

When Jesus died 'the curtain of the temple was torn in two, from top to bottom'.[1]

This was a divine, not a humanly-orchestrated, action ('from top to bottom'). In one sense it was the desecration of the temple. The moment Jesus died was the moment God ceased to have any use for it. Its function throughout the centuries had now been fulfilled. It became de-consecrated ground.

If this was the curtain that separated off the holy of holies, it hid from human view the one room on earth that represented the presence of God. Only once a year, and that briefly, and carrying sacrificial blood, was one man, the Jewish High Priest, allowed beyond that curtain. For this was the earthly throne room of the invisible God. The curtain said, 'You dare not come in.'

Now a greater sacrifice had been made – the sacrifice of God's only Son on the cross, sufficient to pardon the sins of any and all who trust in him. No other sacrifice will ever be needed. Now the heavenly Father, not in sorrow, but in the welcome of the gospel, tore the veil that hid him from us and barred sinners from entering his holy presence. Now the rending of the curtain tells us, 'Through faith in the pardon-bringing sacrifice of my Son all your sins are forgiven. You are now a welcome guest in my presence, an adopted and loved child in my family.'

Mark records a fascinating pattern as he unfolds the events of these last hours of Jesus' life. It is not altogether clear whether he did this consciously, or whether it happened under the direction of the Holy Spirit without Mark fully realizing it. Just at the end of his Gospel proclamation, he brings forward out of the shadows, it seems from nowhere, three individuals.

These three people never reappear in the New Testament. They flash across the horizon like meteors and then disappear. None of them is a key figure in the narrative. What they share in common is the way

[1] Mark 15:38.

each of them could say something important to us about the cross, commentaries that lead us to the heart of what it means.

• *Barabbas* was the 'son of a father' who, because of the death of the Son of the heavenly Father was set free. Jesus died in his place. If someone said to him, 'How is it that you, a man condemned to die now live despite your sins?' Barabbas could say, 'Because Jesus died in my place. He took my place and was condemned; my pardon was sealed by the shedding of his blood.'

• *Simon of Cyrene* whose boys are named by Mark, might have been asked, 'What did you see in the crucifixion of Jesus?' and could have replied, 'I saw in the crucifixion of Jesus the meaning of his words, "If anyone would come after me, let him deny himself and take up his cross daily and follow me."'[1]

• *A Roman Centurion* was in charge of the execution squad – a death specialist. Who knows how many executions he had overseen? Who knows what dark and disturbing flashback dreams he may have had because of his obedience to his commanding officer? 'Sir', we might ask, 'What did you see that afternoon so long ago?' Surely he could reply: 'I saw in the way he died that this man was none other than the Son of God.'[2]

Truly,

> In my place condemned he stood
> Sealed my pardon with his blood.

Would that all the world would grasp this and sing in response,

> Hallelujah! what a Saviour!

I may share that hope, but I am not personally responsible for how the whole world responds to Jesus Christ. There is, however, one person's response for which I have sole and total responsibility – my own. Have I seen that the meaning of the cross belongs to the things that Paul said are of 'first importance' for me: that 'Christ died for our sins in accordance with the Scriptures'?[3] Can I say 'Bearing shame –

[1] Luke 9:23.
[2] Mark 15:39.
[3] 1 Corinthians 15:3.

my shame – and scoffing rude, in *my* place condemned he stood and sealed *my* pardon with his blood'? If so, then I will want to shout:

Hallelujah! what a Saviour!

Yes, indeed, What a Saviour!

7. The Tomb – *Resurrection*

Who is He, that from the grave
Comes to heal, and help, and save?

'Tis the Lord! O wondrous story!
'Tis the Lord! the King of glory!
At His feet we humbly fall;
Crown Him, Crown Him Lord of all.

John 20:1-23

Now on the first day of the week Mary Magdalene came to the tomb early, while it was still dark, and saw that the stone had been taken away from the tomb. ² So she ran and went to Simon Peter and the other disciple, the one whom Jesus loved, and said to them, 'They have taken the Lord out of the tomb, and we do not know where they have laid him.' ³ So Peter went out with the other disciple, and they were going toward the tomb. ⁴ Both of them were running together, but the other disciple outran Peter and reached the tomb first. ⁵ And stooping to look in, he saw the linen cloths lying there, but he did not go in. ⁶ Then Simon Peter came, following him, and went into the tomb. He saw the linen cloths lying there, ⁷ and the face cloth, which had been on Jesus' head, not lying with the linen cloths but folded up in a place by itself. ⁸ Then the other disciple, who had reached the tomb first, also went in, and he saw and believed; ⁹ for as yet they did not understand the Scripture, that he must rise from the dead. ¹⁰ Then the disciples went back to their homes.

¹¹ But Mary stood weeping outside the tomb, and as she wept she stooped to look into the tomb. ¹² And she saw two angels in white, sitting where the body of Jesus had lain, one at the head and one at the feet. ¹³ They said to her, 'Woman, why are you weeping?' She said to them, 'They have taken away my Lord, and I do not know where they have laid him.' ¹⁴ Having said this, she turned around and saw Jesus standing, but she did not know that it was Jesus. ¹⁵ Jesus said to her, 'Woman, why are you weeping? Whom are you seeking?' Supposing him to be the gardener, she said to him, 'Sir, if you have carried him away, tell me where you have laid him, and I will take him away.' ¹⁶ Jesus said to her, 'Mary.' She turned and said to him in Aramaic, 'Rabboni!' (which means Teacher). ¹⁷ Jesus said to her, 'Do not cling to me, for I have not yet ascended to the Father; but go to my brothers and say to them, "I am ascending to my Father and your Father, to my God and your God."' ¹⁸ Mary Magdalene went and announced to the disciples, 'I have seen the Lord' – and that he had said these things to her.

[19] On the evening of that day, the first day of the week, the doors being locked where the disciples were for fear of the Jews, Jesus came and stood among them and said to them, 'Peace be with you.' [20] When he had said this, he showed them his hands and his side. Then the disciples were glad when they saw the Lord. [21] Jesus said to them again, 'Peace be with you. As the Father has sent me, even so I am sending you.' [22] And when he had said this, he breathed on them and said to them, 'Reccive the Holy Spirit. [23] If you forgive the sins of anyone, they are forgiven; if you withhold forgiveness from anyone, it is withheld.'

Authentic Christianity – the Christianity of Christ and the apostles – is supernatural Christianity. It is not a tame and harmless ethic, consisting of a few moral platitudes, spiced with a dash of religion. It is a resurrection religion, a life lived by the power of God.[1]

IN these words John R. W. Stott echoes what the Apostle Paul included in his list of what is *'of first importance'* in the message of the gospel:

Christ died for our sins in accordance with the Scriptures, that he was buried, that he was raised on the third day in accordance with the Scriptures.[2]

So the notion of a bodily (that is a *physical*) resurrection from the dead lies at the very heart of Christianity. Indeed without this there would be no biblical Christianity, no gospel, and no world-wide and eternity-long family of God, the church.

Yet all this was still to come for Jesus' disciples as they staggered through the first hours following his crucifixion. For all they loved him they did not even have the privilege of burying their Master themselves.[3]

We can only guess at what was going through their minds that Friday evening as they went their separate ways to their lodgings. Some of them probably went to houses in Jerusalem. Others probably went back to Bethany, a few miles away. A dark cloud was now hanging over them. They felt no expectation that something greater than what had recently happened to Lazarus[4] would happen to Jesus within the next two days.

[1] J. R. W. Stott, *Christ the Controversialist* (Downers Grove: Inter-Varsity Press, 1970), 63.
[2] 1 Corinthians 15:3-4.
[3] See John 19:38-42.
[4] See John 11:1-57.

The following day – Saturday – must have been the darkest and most difficult Sabbath imaginable for them. Their whole beings were, doubtless, numbed by what they had seen; but their minds – how could they possibly rest? Paralysis. Fear. Who knows what self-recriminations they all experienced? And in addition, were they also overwhelmed by the thought that the past three years had been for nothing? Had they perhaps been duped as much by themselves as by the Lord Jesus? What use now his carefully memorized sayings?

It is hard to imagine. It is one of many things we might like to ask the disciples: 'What exactly were you thinking?'

What exactly were they doing? Probably not a great deal. A sense of overwhelming despair, disappointment and grief affects us not only emotionally but physically. It produces a kind of inertia.

Jesus' disciples were going through the first stages of grief. Some of them at least had witnessed his crucifixion. Perhaps others had left before he had finally died, unable to bear the strain and agony of watching. But all of them knew that he was dead. And they knew he had been buried in the tomb of the rich man, Joseph of Arimathaea. But at the end of the Sabbath, as darkness fell and the first day of a new week began,[1] did they at last get to bed, having scarcely if at all slept on the Friday night?

Now that Sabbath was over, and a new week was beginning, what were they going to do? Return to Galilee and pick up the pieces of their former lives? The one who had brought them together (and kept them together, despite everything) was gone. Would their friendship, comradeship, love, and their sense that they had been caught up in something much bigger and grander than themselves, all simply disintegrate? Would Peter the fisherman, Matthew the tax collector, Simon the zealot all go their separate ways, wondering what they had ever seen in each other to live and work together for several years?

We know that later on Peter wondered if he should simply try his hand again at fishing. Where now the thrill of being ambassadors of Jesus going through the villages, proclaiming the kingdom, casting out demons, and healing the sick in his name?[2] Had it all been some kind of strange delusion?

[1] The day, including the Sabbath, was measured from sundown to sundown, not from midnight to midnight as we now do.
[2] Luke 9:1-6.

Whatever was going through the minds of the disciples, the discovery of the empty tomb set in motion a change to everything – absolutely everything.

In the decades that followed there were many messianic movements each with its self-appointed messiah. Most of those leaders were killed. The movements they began all collapsed and came to nothing. The followers of these movements went home, and that was that. But if you asked someone, say twenty years on from the death of Jesus, 'Why are you a Christian?' they would most assuredly have answered, 'ἠγέρθη ὁ Κύριος – *the Lord is risen*. Because of Jesus' resurrection.'[1]

An event in history

The resurrection was an event in history, or it was nothing. It is a fact, or it is a fiction.

The New Testament unequivocally regards the resurrection as a fact. There were eye-witnesses. You could have gone to them and said, 'Tell me again about the time that you saw Jesus after he had been raised from the dead. Tell me about the time he spoke to you, and what you said to him. You saw him, didn't you?'

You could have gone to Galilee and done this. Paul tells us – writing to the Corinthians around the middle of the first century – that on one occasion at least five hundred people saw him.[2] He knew for a fact that many of them were still alive. Twenty years after the death of Jesus there were eye-witnesses you could have asked, 'Why are you a Christian?' and the answer would have been the same 'ἠγέρθη ὁ Κύριος – *the Lord is risen!* I am a Christian because of the resurrection!'

This resurrection is an historical event. But we live in a time when people are suspicious of history, and doubt that there really are 'historical facts'. What is usually called 'Post-modernity', like evolutionary philosophy before it, has affected the way we think about everything.

It has affected our view of language (literature now has no fixed meaning; the reader finds his or her own meaning, whatever the author thought he or she was writing). But this, in turn, has affected the modern approach to, and understanding of, history. Thus many writers today are sceptical that you can really know the past. All you

[1] Luke 24:34.
[2] 1 Corinthians 15:6.

can know are people's opinions about the past. It is all very individual, relative, and very fragile. This scepticism has impacted the academic world and flowed over far beyond it.

Christianity is a religion about facts. It is rooted in the fact of a physical resurrection. Without that Christianity collapses. It is altogether destroyed. 'If Christ has not been raised', says Paul, 'your faith is futile.'[1] It is useless.

In the 1990s Barbara Thiering, an Australian academic theologian, was for a short time a popular author. She wrote a couple of bestsellers of a racy 'historical novelette' kind, and as a result she was made a 'fellow' of the infamous 'Jesus Seminar'.[2]

Dr Thiering put forward the thesis that Jesus did not die. One of the two thieves on either side of him was in fact a doctor and gave Jesus a pharmaceutical so that he never actually died. Jesus then travelled with the Apostle Paul and married and had children and – just by the way – also wrote the Gospel of John.

There is not a single shred of evidence for any of this, and of course much testimony against it. Yet her work became a bestseller. People read this without blinking an eye!

Adopting such scepticism about orthodox Christianity is simply one of the many baneful effects of post-modernity. In 2007 James Cameron (director of the famous movie *Titanic*) made a documentary on an ossuary[3] excavated in Jerusalem in 1980. It had the name on it 'Jesus son of Joseph'. Then, lo and behold, they discovered another ossuary with the inscription 'Mariamne' or 'Mary'. And one with the name 'Judah, son of Jesua'. The rest of the story, as they say, is history! The question that excited all the attention was, of course, 'Are these the bones of Jesus? Did he indeed marry and have children? And therefore is the New Testament a fiction?'

[1] 1 Corinthians 15:17.

[2] 'The Jesus Seminar' was founded in 1985 and consisted of a group of about one hundred and fifty scholars who voted on the historicity or otherwise of the contents of the Gospels – always from the basically sceptical presupposition that the burden of proof lay with anyone who held anything in the Gospels to be authentic – a standard of criticism employed in the study of no other historical document.

[3] An ossuary is a container in which are kept the bones of a body whose soft tissue has decayed. These ossuaries, being smaller than caskets, meant that a single tomb could hold the remains of a considerable number of people.

Significantly those who were least impressed by the documentary were the Jewish scholars who had discovered the ossuaries, and for a very simple reason: they, of all people, knew that there were thousands of people called 'Jesus' in the history of Judaism. Jesus is the name 'Joshua'; and there were multitudes of men in the first century called 'Joshua/Jesus'. The find was no more unusual than finding 'Thomas' in a Welsh telephone directory, or 'Ferguson' in a Scottish one! Yet we live in an age when people *prefer* to believe there must be something in this sensationalism rather than give any credence to the testimony of hundreds of eye-witnesses.

Now, if Paul tells us the bodily resurrection of Jesus from the dead is so important that if it turns out not to be true 'we are of all people most to be pitied',[1] we are surely wise, objective, and fair-minded *only* if we are prepared to listen to the testimony of those who were eye-witnesses.

In this context we will focus on a single account of the resurrection. We have chosen the account in the Gospel of John.[2] Its focus is on Mary Magdalene, Simon Peter, and John, and the events that happened on that first Easter Sunday from morning until evening.

A fact

Jesus was dead. This was the case – however you define death: your heart stops beating, there are no brain waves. Whatever the current scientific test of death might be, Jesus was dead. For one thing the crucifixion squad of Roman soldiers were clearly seasoned executioners. You do not play dice underneath a gibbet unless you have become hardened to what is happening within a few feet of your indifference. If there was any doubt, one of the soldiers made sure he was dead by thrusting a spear into Jesus' side. And John, perhaps for more than one reason, recorded that blood and water flowed out.[3] John himself was there. He saw it with his own eyes. He was a witness to the death of Jesus.[4]

[1] 1 Corinthians 15:19.

[2] John 20:1-31.

[3] John 19:35.

[4] For an in-depth assessment of the many attempts to disparage the historicity of the resurrection of Christ, see Gary R. Habermas and Michael R. Licona, *The Case for the Resurrection of Jesus* (Grand Rapids: Kregel, 2004), and Richard Bauckham,

Because it was the evening of the Sabbath, and Passover time to boot, a speedy burial was desired by the Jews.[1] It was a sad commentary on their priorities; having had an innocent man crucified they now fussed over liturgical details.

Thus a quick, and temporary burial was arranged. The completion of the burial rites could wait until Sunday morning. Pilate gave permission for the body of Jesus to be taken down and to be placed in the tomb of Joseph of Arimathea so that he would be buried before the Sabbath.

Two leading figures in Jewish circles, Joseph himself and Nicodemus, witnessed the burial. They placed Jesus' lifeless body in a shroud, binding it in linen cloths, with separate bandages around the head, carefully packing the substantial amount of myrrh and aloes that Nicodemus had brought for the occasion. There was a lavish amount of spices – 'one hundred *litras*', John tells us, or about seventy-five pounds in weight.[2] It was enough for a king's burial, and all used to help slow down the putrefaction process.

Jesus was probably laid on a ledge in this newly-hewn tomb. Perhaps a year or so later, if all were well, his bones could have been put in an ossuary.

That was the intention; no one was expecting, and certainly neither Joseph nor Nicodemus was preparing him for a resurrection.

Everything John tells us underlines one simple fact: *Jesus was dead* and, in whatever haste, he had been carefully buried. The Roman soldiers confirmed it; the Jews confirmed it; Joseph of Arimathea confirmed it; Nicodemus ('*the* teacher of Israel', according to Jesus himself[3]) confirmed it. John is telling us he was dead and that nobody was expecting a resurrection. We might well borrow the words of the High Priest the previous night, 'What further witnesses do we need?'[4]

John had been with Jesus for three years. He had repeatedly heard him say that on the third day he would rise again.[5] This is his story,

---

Jesus and the Eyewitnesses: The Gospels as Eyewitness Testimony (Grand Rapids: Wm B. Eerdmans, 2006).

[1] John 19:31.
[2] John 19:39.
[3] John 3:10.
[4] Mark 14:63.
[5] Mark 8:31; 9:31; 10:34.

told from his own perspective. How he records it is of special interest partly because of the way he focuses on the experience of Mary Magdalene.

The dawn treaders

Several women came to the tomb early that Sunday morning, just as dawn was about to break.[1]

Perhaps Mary set out from her home when it was still dark and by the time she arrived at the tomb morning light had begun to break. We all have had the experience of getting up early in the morning when it is dark outside, engaging in some activity or other, and then – all of a sudden – daylight is upon us. In certain parts of the world the transition is very rapid. It gets dark very quickly and it gets light very quickly. Perhaps this is why one Gospel writer says it was dark while another speaks of it as being light – they are simply speaking from different perspectives. So it was probably dark when Mary Magdalene *began* her journey to the tomb and it was light *at the end of it* when she arrived at it.

Earlier it seems Mary had not been on her own. She herself hints at this when she says to Peter and John, 'They have taken the Lord out of the tomb, and *we* do not know where they have laid him.'[2] John was doubtless aware that there were others; but he is focusing here only on Mary Magdalene.

If you were making up this Gospel – and of course there have long been suggestions that this is essentially what John did – there is one thing you would *not* do at this point.

What is that? You would certainly not have indicated that the first witness of the risen Christ was Mary Magdalene.

Is this because Simon Peter is the apostle who is always mentioned first in any and every list of the disciples? Or because John would thereby compromise his repeated claim to be 'the disciple whom Jesus loved'? Or is it, perhaps, because Mary Magdalene has so often been identified with the 'sinner' of Luke 7:36-50 – almost certainly mistakenly?

No, the reason is quite different, much more straightforward, and much less subtle: *Mary was a woman*. By first-century Jewish standards

[1] For example, Mark 16:1ff.
[2] John 20:2.

her evidence would have been regarded as legally inadmissible. The only reason, therefore, for its inclusion by John was the obvious one. It was true.

When Mary arrived at the tomb she saw the stone rolled away and jumped to the only reasonable conclusion: 'His body has been stolen.' In her state of mind grave robbers seemed a more plausible explanation than divine power.

In fact this possibility had already been anticipated by the Sanhedrin.[1] They warned Pilate that Jesus' disciples might raid the tomb, steal the body, and then claim that he had risen. Paradoxically they seemed to have a better memory of Jesus' teaching than the disciples themselves!

In any event, Mary Magdalene shares the same conclusion as all of the other women when she sees the tomb opened: somebody must have taken the body. So she runs to tell Peter and John, the two most prominent disciples. They in turn now set off at speed for the tomb, leaving Mary Magdalene following behind.

Peter and John

Just at this point John includes a little detail that underlines that what we have here is an authentic eye-witness account. It really does nothing to advance the story, yet at the same time explains an element in it. John *outran* Peter. Was this the now much older man looking back on his younger days and remembering that their long-standing friendship also had a touch of inbuilt rivalry ('Ah, in those days I could even outrun Peter!')?[2] Whatever the catalyst for its inclusion, it corroborates the sense of historical authenticity.

But although John reached the tomb before Peter he did not go directly into it. He simply peered in. But then Peter arrived and went straight inside. So like Peter! But what does he see? The very same objects John had seen – perhaps the very sight of them had made him hesitate to take a step further: 'the linen cloths lying there'. But then John adds, 'and the face cloth which had been on Jesus' head, not lying with the linen cloths but *folded up in a place by itself*.'[3]

[1] Matthew 27:62-66. The Sanhedrin was the Jewish Ruling Council.
[2] The narrative in John 21:20-23 may also suggest this. If so, it is moving to think that the aged John would have known that his boyhood friend and disciple companion had paid the ultimate price of being a disciple, whereas he was still alive.
[3] John 20:6-7.

It is possible to interpret these last words in more than one way. Perhaps John means that only Peter saw the cloth that had been around Jesus' face, heavy with the spices smeared in between its weaves. It was folded up and positioned in a separate place from the other cloths.

Or maybe – and this is perhaps the more obvious interpretation – there was simply a little space between the head and the rest of the body, where the neck had been. In that case John probably had seen both, but perhaps without registering the significance of what he was seeing until a few minutes later when he entered the tomb – and believed.

If you had been a watcher within the tomb during the night hours between that Passover Sabbath and Easter Sunday morning, what would you have seen? Jesus is heavily wrapped up, perhaps almost doubling the size of his body with all the bandages and spices. Would you have seen movement within this shroud? Or would you have witnessed a mystery – the transformation of his mortal body into his resurrection body? Would the grave clothes simply have seemed to deflate – and then a resurrected body appear – recognizably the same, and yet with new powers fit for a new mode of existence?

We know from the resurrection narratives that Jesus' resurrected body was a physical body – a body that walked, spoke, and that could eat fish.[1] It was a real body; a breathing body; presumably a body that was warm to touch. Yet it could appear and disappear. That same evening it would appear in a room where the doors were locked.[2] Presumably John meant us to draw the obvious conclusion: they did not unlock the door in order to let Jesus in. He simply appeared in the room. His physical body is now a resurrection body. It has new, yet wonderfully human, properties.

So John is describing what he and Peter saw. It is as if he is giving evidence in a court of law:

> *Question*: 'Did you see anything when you arrived at the tomb?'
> *Answer*: 'Yes, I did.'

[1] Luke 24:42-3.
[2] John 20:19.

Question: 'Will you describe it in detail? Please tell us exactly what you saw.'
Answer: 'I saw the head bandages were separated from the rest of the bandages.'

Question: 'Did this remind you of what you saw when your friend Lazarus of Bethany came out of his tomb?'
Answer: 'No. It wasn't actually like Lazarus at all. You see, when Lazarus came out, all the death-bandages were still wrapped around him. It was a struggle for him to move, so Jesus told us to unwrap the bandages. It wasn't at all like that with Jesus. It looked as though he had simply come out *through* the bandages.'

Question: 'Well, can you describe this in other terms to help us to understand what you saw?'
Answer: 'Perhaps the best way I can describe it is this: It was clear to me that Lazarus had experienced a *resuscitation*. Obviously something remarkable had happened to him. But he was exactly the same man he had been before he "died". In that respect nothing about him was different. But when I looked into the tomb of Jesus I knew immediately that this was not a *resuscitation* but a *resurrection*. Whatever had happened to Jesus he had not simply come back to the same old life again. He had entered into a new kind of life.'

Peter and John were in no state to construct a theology of the resurrection. But what they have described is clear enough – and John enables us to see it through their eyes – to convince us that what happened was not a grave robbery but a resurrection.

And so Peter and John make their way back home, and momentarily disappear from the scene. As yet they have not seen the risen Christ.

Mary Magdalene

But now Mary Magdalene steps on to centre stage.

Perhaps the two apostles emerged from the tomb, met Mary and said to her, 'We're going back to the disciples, something remarkable has happened.' It would be perfectly understandable if they were reluctant to tell her what they were thinking. How could they say 'We think Jesus has been raised from the dead' and then simply leave her on her own?

John's narrative continues, but now events are narrated as though we could see them through Mary's eyes:

Mary is looking into the tomb.

She sees two 'people' – without realizing they are angels.

They are speaking to her: 'Why are you weeping?'

She's crying. She still thinks somebody has stolen the body, and taken it away.

But then she hears another voice, this time coming from behind her.

She turns round and sees a third figure. It must be the gardener.

Mary did think it was *the gardener*. This can hardly be an insignificant detail. Why did John not simply say, 'But at first she didn't realize it was Jesus'? Is he telling us something that even Mary herself didn't quite grasp?

John began his Gospel by echoing the creation narrative in Genesis chapter 1: 'In the beginning was the Word ... all things were made through him ...'[1] Jesus was the Creator of the cosmos, and the one who planted the garden in Eden, and then called Adam to be its gardener, extending its boundaries to the ends of the earth.[2]

Now at the beginning of the new creation, Mary mistook Jesus for a gardener. Perhaps, after all, it was not a mistake. For the Word had become flesh; the Creator had become the Second Man, appointed to do the work which the first gardener, Adam, had so signally failed to do. He had risen from the old world of death in order to do his work of restoration by replanting this fallen world and beginning a new creation that would eventually become a glorious garden.[3]

Through her tears Mary bravely remonstrates with the stranger. The dialogue is as realistic as it is poignant: 'Look, if you've taken the body, tell me where you have laid him and I will take him away.' She is so sweet, so grief-stricken, so eager and determined, so confused. She is physically incapable of even attempting to 'take him away' – yet

---

[1] John 1:1, 3.

[2] Genesis 2:8.

[3] Notice how John saw this fulfilled in Revelation 21–22. When God makes all things 'new' (Revelation 21:5), the final destiny of the world is simultaneously (1) a new heaven and a new earth; (2) a new city, the new Jerusalem; (3) a cosmic temple where the glory of God is everywhere manifested; and (4) a new Eden, cultivated to perfection (Revelation 22:1–5).

determined that he should be honoured. But notice too how biblical her words are. She continues to refer to 'him' and not to 'it'.

Why did she not recognize Jesus? Maybe the sun was shining in her eyes? Perhaps in those early hours of the day there was a shadow cast over him? Or perhaps the tears were misting her vision? Or perhaps she was overtaken with a sense of grief that seemed to make everyone and everything dull, unimportant, scarcely worth noticing? After all, her entire focus was on what had happened to Jesus, not on who this gardener might be.

Or was she not really looking at him, as John's account seems to suggest, because when he speaks again she 'turned, and said ...'?[1] This too breathes reality and authenticity.

And then, again, this is Jesus in his resurrected body. Did that make a difference? We can only guess.

Jesus, the gardener, speaks her name, 'Mary'. She knows that voice! Can it really be ...? As instinctively as we recognize the voice of a loved one on the phone she now recognizes him. It is just as the Saviour had said about the shepherd: 'the sheep hear his voice, and he calls his own sheep by name'.[2]

The first person to see the risen Lord Jesus was a woman.

Throughout this whole section John has made it clear that the disciples were not expecting a resurrection. In the event it was as incredible to them as it is to modern man. Far from being gullible – uneducated, and unscientific – and therefore inclined to believe in Jesus' resurrection, the facts point in the opposite direction.

The disciples were not expecting a resurrection *at all* – and for the same reasons modern people are sceptical: they 'knew' that dead people do not rise. The dead stay dead. This was not only the view in the Hellenistic world in which the first Christians lived; the major Jewish sect of the Sadducees did not believe in a personal resurrection either (and thought they could show that it was an absurd idea).[3]

Even those who did believe in the resurrection, like Lazarus's sister Martha, were certainly not expecting it to happen any time soon. Yes, Lazarus would rise – but only on the last day.[4]

[1] John 20:16.
[2] John 10:3.
[3] Matthew 22:23-33.
[4] John 11:24.

So Mary Magdalene was not expecting a resurrection here and now, and certainly not a personal, physical resurrection. Indeed she can scarcely take it in. All she knows is that Jesus is back; he is there, standing in front of her. It isn't his ghost, is it? It is Jesus, isn't it? She grabs hold of him. She thought he was gone forever, but now he is here. She will not let him go again! She wants to hold on to him forever. Here he was physically. But he had been there physically before and had been snatched away. Never again!

Notice in passing just how physical the resurrected Jesus is. He can be held on to, and gripped tight. His body had shape and form. This is not the spirit of Jesus living on. This is Jesus resurrected.

John Dominic Crossan became well known as one of the leading figures in 'The Jesus Seminar' famous for its verdicts on the authenticity or otherwise of all the elements in the Gospel narrative. Since miracles 'cannot happen', passages that refer to one are easily dismissed. Professor Crossan suggests that Jesus was buried in a shallow grave and wild dogs ate him. As far as he is concerned Easter was just a feeling on Peter's part, a 'sense' that came over him. But John's account is a whole diameter removed from that. What Dr Crossan cannot touch, see, measure, or believe in, Mary Magdalene could touch and hold. In this instance we throw in our lot with the eye-witnesses.

Jesus gently tells Mary not to hold on to him in this way. The reason is intriguing: 'I have not yet ascended.'

This is a simple statement with profound significance.

The resurrection of Jesus is in fact *part one* of the two-stage process of his exaltation. Subsequent to his resurrection – as we will see in the next chapter – his ascension to the right hand of his Father took place. Mary must not cling to him, as though he had simply been resuscitated so that his former life can continue more or less as it was – just like Lazarus. No, he has begun his exaltation. She must learn the lesson Jesus had already taught the apostles in the upper room: he was going to leave them – but that would be to their advantage. Only then would he send his Spirit to indwell and empower them.[1]

How much of this Mary understood immediately we have no way of telling. But then Jesus adds: 'Do not cling to me ... but go to my brothers and say to them, "I am ascending to my Father and your

[1] John 16:7-11.

Father, to my God and your God.'" She is to be his messenger to tell the apostles that the promise he had given them in the upper room was now coming true. He would not leave them as orphans! They are being adopted as the children of God, as his *brothers*. They are family now. His God is their God; his Father is theirs too.[1]

There is no complete agreement about the precise meaning of these words. Often they have been interpreted as though Jesus were distinguishing between his relationship to God and that of the disciples – as though God were his God and Father in one sense and his disciples' God and Father in another sense. But the better – and more natural – interpretation is surely the opposite. He is drawing them into the privileges of which he had spoken only three evenings before. Now all who trust in him and belong to him are his brothers. In and through the risen Son they are adopted into the family of God, and he is their Father![2]

These, then, are the basic facts of the resurrection. And the first person to discover its wonder was a woman, Mary Magdalene. And as we have hinted, what makes this both so astonishing *and* at the same time so authenticating is that in the context of the first century, women could not testify in court. Their testimony was inadmissible. That was the culture – it was not the idea of the apostles or the early Christians! But this simply underlines the reliability and historicity of John's account of the resurrection. If he had fabricated it the last thing he would be likely to include was that the first person who saw the risen Jesus was a woman.

This, then, is how it happened.

Significance

It takes the rest of the New Testament to explore and explain the full significance of Jesus' resurrection. After all, not a single syllable of it was written *before* the resurrection. In this sense the resurrection is the cause of the New Testament, and its *sine qua non* – no resurrection, no New Testament.

But within the confines of this one section of the Easter story John has woven into his account some very important teaching.

[1] John 20:17. Cf. 14:18.
[2] For a similar perspective see Hebrews 2:11-12, 14-17; Romans 8:16-17, 29.

John tells us that 'the other disciple [that is John himself], who had reached the tomb first, also went in, and he saw and believed.'

'*He saw and believed.*' We cannot be quite sure about Peter at this point; but certainly John has come to believe in the resurrected Christ – as a result of seeing the grave clothes lying there.

Notice, however, how John explains that he had not yet put it all together with the teaching of the Old Testament – for 'as yet they did not understand the Scripture that he must rise from the dead'.[1]

John knew Psalm 16, for example, which stated that the Lord would not let his 'holy one see corruption'.[2] He had heard the Lord quote Psalm 22 on the cross – and while it begins with the agony of his sense of God-forsakenness, it ends in victory and triumph. But he was not yet at the stage of remembering the promises of the Old Testament. He could scarcely take in that the promises he had heard from Jesus about the resurrection had been true!

John did not yet understand how the whole Old Testament pointed to Jesus. Later the Saviour would teach him and the others how this was so. But he had grasped the significance of the grave clothes and the empty tomb. His Gospel is a book of signs – indeed he tells us that there were 'many other signs' that Jesus did 'in the presence of his disciples, which are not written in this book; but these are written so that you may believe'.[3] This is one of those signs. The folded grave clothes and the empty tomb constitute the first sign that Jesus has conquered death and the grave. He has gained the victory. He has dealt with our sin and guilt; he has, as he promised 'cast out' the evil one, 'the ruler of this world'.[4] And John believed.

Victory

Every Sunday, in many churches throughout the world, the Apostles' Creed is confessed in unison by the whole congregation.

The Creed is an ancient summary of the Christian gospel. In it Christians confess their faith in the Father as the Creator, the Son as the Redeemer, and the Holy Spirit. They also celebrate the privileges of

[1] John 20:9.
[2] Psalm 16:10.
[3] John 20:30.
[4] John 12:31.

belonging to the fellowship of the church, the blessings of the gospel, and the end of the world.[1]

The Creed tells us that Jesus Christ 'descended into hell'. The expression has been variously understood. But it surely reminds us, among other elements, that on the cross Jesus engaged the powers of darkness. Paul tells us he disarmed them and triumphed over them. In his own hours of shame he 'put them to open shame, by triumphing over them'.[2] John himself says elsewhere: 'The reason the Son of God appeared was to destroy the works of the devil.'[3] The empty tomb was the first sign that this battle with the forces of darkness had not only been engaged, but that in it Christ had triumphed. In Peter's words on the Day of Pentecost, 'God raised him up, loosing the pangs of death, because it was not possible for him to be held by it … he was not abandoned to Hades …'[4] The empty tomb was a sign of his victory – over sin, and death, and hell. The implication is that Satan can now never triumph over someone who has sought and found refuge in the resurrected Christ.

---

[1] Although not written by the apostles themselves, the Apostles' Creed has served the church throughout the centuries as a summary of apostolic teaching:

'I believe in God the Father, Almighty,
Maker of heaven and earth;
And in Jesus Christ, his only Son, our Lord,
Who was conceived by the Holy Ghost,
Born of the Virgin Mary;
Suffered under Pontius Pilate,
Was crucified, dead and buried;
He descended into hell.
The third day he rose again from the dead.
He ascended into heaven,
And sits at the right hand of God the Father Almighty.
From thence he shall come to judge the quick and the dead.
I believe in the Holy Ghost,
The holy catholic church,
The communion of saints,
The forgiveness of sins,
The resurrection of the body,
And the life everlasting. Amen.'

[2] Colossians 2:15.
[3] 1 John 3:8.
[4] Acts 2:24.

'Who is to condemn? Christ Jesus is the one who died – more than that, who was raised ...'.[1]

Justification

John Bunyan's *Pilgrim's Progress* records a dramatic scene in which Christian, the Pilgrim, is confronted by Apollyon, the devil. Apollyon condemns him as utterly unworthy of the name of Christian. How was the Pilgrim to respond? How is any Christian to respond?

The Pilgrim replies,

> All this is true, and much more, which thou hast left out; but the Prince whom I serve and honour, is merciful, and ready to forgive ... [I] have obtained Pardon of my Prince.[2]

In essence he is saying, 'You don't even know the half of my sin and failure. I am much worse than you think. But I am not trusting in my own righteousness, nor in my own power to conquer you. I am trusting in the righteousness and power of my prince Jesus, who died and rose again to bring me forgiveness and to conquer you and all his and my enemies!'

John Newton well understood this, and taught his congregation to sing:

> Bowed down beneath a load of sin,
>   By Satan sorely pressed,
> By war without and fears within,
>   I come to Thee for rest.
>
> Be Thou my shield and hiding-place,
>   That, sheltered near Thy side,
> I may my fierce accuser face,
>   And tell him Thou hast died.[3]

Yes, tell Satan that Christ died for you. Tell him that he rose again for your justification. Tell him that because you are 'in Christ' you are accounted by God as being as righteous in his sight as Jesus himself

---

[1] Romans 8:34.

[2] John Bunyan, *The Pilgrim's Progress*, Edited with an Introduction and Notes by N.H. Keeble (Oxford: Oxford University Press, 1984), 48.

[3] From the hymn by John Newton (1725–1807), 'Approach, my soul, the mercy-seat.'

– because you are counted righteous with Jesus' own righteousness!

> Jesus, Thy blood and righteousness
>> My beauty are, my glorious dress;
> 'Midst flaming worlds, in these arrayed,
>> With joy shall I lift up my head.
>
> Bold shall I stand in that great day;
>> For who aught to my charge shall lay?
> Fully absolved through Thee I am,
>> From sin and fear, from guilt and shame.[1]

All this flows, ultimately from the resurrection, for '… Jesus our Lord … was delivered up for our trespasses *and raised for our justification.*'[2]

John 'believed'. His testimony prompts the question: 'Do I believe too? Do I believe in Jesus, risen from the dead, conqueror of hell and the grave?'

Think of all that sin and death do to us. Their influence lies behind all manner of physical ailments, sorrows and disappointments, and every kind of fear. And if sin is our constant enemy, then death is the *'last* enemy'.[3] But the day is coming when, in a new and glorious resurrection body, the lame will leap, the deaf will hear the sound of the Saviour's voice, the blind will see his face, the sick will be healed, and every tear will be wiped out of our eyes by God himself. And all of this is a consequence of the resurrection of Jesus.

Peace

But John tells us that Jesus did something else that first Easter Sunday. In the evening he appeared to the disciples who were together in a room, perhaps in the same room in which they had last talked with him. Fearful that those responsible for Jesus' crucifixion might now turn on them, they had locked the doors of the house.[4] But they could not lock Jesus out! He appeared in the room.

[1] From the hymn by Nikolaus L. von Zinzendorf (1700–60) *'Christi Blut und Gerechtigkeit'*, translated by John Wesley.

[2] Romans 4:25.

[3] 1 Corinthians 15:26.

[4] John 20:19.

Jesus did something – or rather said something – that was enormously significant to these Jewish disciples. His first word was a benediction: '*Shalom*' he said; 'Peace be with you.' The word signified wholeness, well-being, complete healing, integration; peace with God, peace with themselves, peace with each other, peace with creation. He had taken the curse; now he was bestowing the blessing. It was just what Isaiah had said the Suffering Servant would accomplish: 'upon him was the chastisement that brought us peace'.[1] Now Jesus was giving them that peace.

The times, as Shakespeare wrote, were 'out of joint'.[2] Still today creation itself continues to groan and travail as though aching for the renewal of all things – for *shalom*.[3] And here Jesus is setting in motion the grand process of restoration. He is our Aaron, our High Priest, coming from the holy of holies where he himself has been the sacrifice for our sins. His appearance is the clear signal that his sacrifice has been accepted by God. His people's sins have been forgiven. He raises his hands and pronounces the Aaronic blessing: 'The Lord bless you ... and give you *shalom*.'[4]

Paul takes this scene and describes it in theological terms: 'Jesus our Lord ... was delivered up for our trespasses and raised for our justification. Therefore, since we have been justified by faith, we have peace with God.' 'He [the risen Christ] came and preached peace to you.'[5] But there is one further note John strikes; it is a note of promise.

The Spirit of Christ

John tells us that when Jesus had said these things to the disciples, he 'breathed on them and said to them, "Receive the Holy Spirit."'[6]

This is a symbolic gesture; an acted parable. 'Breath' and 'spirit' are the same word in both Hebrew and Greek (*ruach* in Hebrew, *pneuma* in Greek). Here the risen Jesus is acting out a drama whose full significance will become clear in the days to come. He is giving them a hint of their future.

[1] Isaiah 53:5.
[2] William Shakespeare, *Hamlet, Prince of Denmark*, Act I, Scene V.
[3] See Romans 8:20-22.
[4] Numbers 6:24-26.
[5] Romans 4:24-5:1. Ephesians 2:17.
[6] John 20:22.

In forty days he will ascend to his throne in the Father's presence. He will send the Holy Spirit, the promised other Counsellor who will be with his disciples forever. This will be the third stage in his exaltation. Christ has been raised; he will ascend; he will distribute the Spirit as his coronation gift to his church. Thus his resurrection is the assurance and guarantee that the Holy Spirit is coming.

But for what purpose will the Spirit come? Jesus explains it to them. He is sending them to the ends of the earth with the message of his resurrection. For this they will need the help of the same Spirit who empowered him. And so he commissions them: 'As the Father sent me, so I send you – receive the Spirit.'[1]

What a wonderful thing it is to be a Christian – to know the risen Christ, to have *shalom* now with God, to enjoy Christ's pardon, restoration, and victory over all of his and our enemies. And in addition to know that his resurrection is the first-fruits whose final harvest will come in our resurrection. We therefore look forward to the regeneration of all things, and the new heavens and new earth which we will experience in resurrection bodies like our Saviour's.

Yes, there is sorrow, and sadness, and parting in death. But the resurrection of Christ means that we do not say a final farewell to those who are Christ's, but only *'adieu'* ('to God [I commit you]), and *'au revoir'* (until we see [one another] again).

But that is not yet. In the meantime, Jesus gives his disciples work to do:

> All authority in heaven and earth has been given to me. Go therefore and make disciples of all nations, baptizing them in the name of the Father and of the Son and of the Holy Spirit, teaching them to observe all that I have commanded you. And behold, I am with you always, to the end of the age.[2]

So the fruit of the resurrection in our lives includes going and telling what we have come to know and believe. But what shall we tell them? Tell them about the empty tomb; tell them about the risen Christ; and tell them how he forgives our sins and transforms our lives now and for all eternity.

[1] John 20:21.
[2] Matthew 28:18-20.

8. The Throne – *Ascension*

Who is He that from His throne
Rules the world of light alone?

> *'Tis the Lord! O wondrous story!*
> *'Tis the Lord! the King of glory!*
> *At His feet we humbly fall;*
> *Crown Him, Crown Him Lord of all.*

Luke 24:50-53

Then he led them out as far as Bethany, and lifting up his hands he blessed them. 51 While he blessed them, he parted from them and was carried up into heaven. 52 And they worshipped him and returned to Jerusalem with great joy, 53 and were continually in the temple blessing God.

Acts 1:1-11

In the first book, O Theophilus, I have dealt with all that Jesus began to do and teach, 2 until the day when he was taken up, after he had given commands through the Holy Spirit to the apostles whom he had chosen. 3 To them he presented himself alive after his suffering by many proofs, appearing to them during forty days and speaking about the kingdom of God. 4 And while staying with them he ordered them not to depart from Jerusalem, but to wait for the promise of the Father, which, he said, 'you heard from me; 5 for John baptized with water, but you will be baptized with the Holy Spirit not many days from now.'

6 So when they had come together, they asked him, 'Lord, will you at this time restore the kingdom to Israel?' 7 He said to them, 'It is not for you to know times or seasons that the Father has fixed by his own authority. 8 But you will receive power when the Holy Spirit has come upon you, and you will be my witnesses in Jerusalem and in all Judea and Samaria, and to the end of the earth.' 9 And when he had said these things, as they were looking on, he was lifted up, and a cloud took him out of their sight. 10 And while they were gazing into heaven as he went, behold, two men stood by them in white robes, 11 and said, 'Men of Galilee, why do you stand looking into heaven? This Jesus, who was taken up from you into heaven, will come in the same way as you saw him go into heaven.'

I N the Apostles' Creed,[1] as we have seen, Christians confess that Jesus Christ is God's only Son who

> Was conceived by the Holy Ghost,
> Born of the Virgin Mary;
> Suffered under Pontius Pilate,
> Was crucified, dead, and buried;
> He descended into hell.
> The third day he rose again from the dead.
> He …

He what? What is the next major event in the ministry of Christ?

> He ascended into heaven,
> And sits at the right hand of God the Father Almighty.

Jesus' ascension to heaven appears in the very earliest forms of the Creed. Yet perhaps this is the most frequently neglected element in Jesus' ministry – except in churches where the 'Christian Year' is followed in the liturgy and Ascension Day is marked.

Why is the ascension important? What is its practical significance?

It is possible that in one sense there may have been a whole series of interim 'ascensions' between Jesus' resurrection and his final farewell. At the garden tomb he had told Mary Magdalene not to hold on to him as though his resurrection was merely a return to the old days. He said, 'I have not yet ascended.' Was he perhaps signalling to Mary that he would return to his Father immediately – but then continue to come back again, at least for a season? In between the resurrection appearances he seems to have disappeared somewhere – but where? He disappeared from the disciples he met on the Emmaus Road after he had broken bread in their presence: 'he vanished from their sight'.[2]

---

[1] See above, p. 124, fn 1.
[2] Luke 24:31.

He appeared later that evening. But then he disappeared again. He appeared at the Sea of Tiberias (Galilee),[1] but there is no record of his movements. Luke tells us that Jesus was 'appearing to them during forty days', 'staying with them' (more literally 'taking salt together' or 'eating with them').[2] We are left with the impression that he came and went in order to prepare them for a final departure.

Luke twice records that final departure.[3] It took place some six weeks after the resurrection, and just prior to the Feast of Pentecost. It was clearly a 'final' ascension to the Father, took place in a decisive way, and left his disciples in no doubt that it marked the end of this brief period of fellowship with him in his resurrected body. This is why Luke, being the historian that he was, recorded the event in some detail, describing how the Saviour ascended visibly and physically and disappeared from sight in a cloud.

We have seen that three of the apostles had witnessed something remarkable happening to Jesus – at his transfiguration. But what they saw now was different: 'he was lifted up, and a cloud took him out of their sight'.[4]

Jesus could, presumably, have returned permanently to the Father in a variety of ways. He could have simply said, 'This is my last visit to you', and left as he did on other occasions. But instead he 'ascends' visibly, before their very eyes. In fact this was such a staggering sight that the disciples stood peering into the sky and were only 'brought back to earth again', as it were, by the question of the 'two men … in white robes' who asked them, 'Men of Galilee, why do you stand looking into heaven?'[5]

But why did Jesus leave them in this way? The simplest answer is probably the right one.

We tend to attach significance to physical movement. We all understand that the 'top' of the class is a preferable position to the 'bottom' of it! As students we were occasionally invited to sit at 'high table' with the faculty. Parents all want to see their children 'go up in the world'. We prefer it when people 'look up to' rather than 'look

[1] John 21:1.
[2] Acts 1: 3-4.
[3] Luke 24:50-53; Acts 1:6-11.
[4] Acts 1:9.
[5] Acts 1: 11.

down on' us. Monarchs 'ascend' to their thrones. People 'go down hill'. Physical movement thus becomes a metaphor expressing status. What better way then for Jesus to show his disciples that he was now 'ascending to the throne' than to be taken up in this triumphant form into heaven?

As the Apostles' Creed goes on to say: 'He sits at the right hand of God the Father Almighty.'

Ascending but returning

Jesus' ascension not only indicated his final disappearance from sight; it also pointed forward to his future visible return in glory.

Luke records the question of the two men in white robes who had appeared after Jesus ascended. 'Why do you stand here looking into heaven?', they asked.[1] Were some disciples still thinking, 'This is amazing – but he's going to come back soon. This is just a temporary disappearance. We aren't sure what this is all about. But he's surely going to come back.'

But Jesus was not going to come back, at least not immediately. The disciples needed to be clear about that, and to remember the instructions he had given them 'not to depart from Jerusalem, but to wait for the promise of the Father'.[2] At the same time they needed to be reminded and reassured that their Lord would return, albeit not yet.

They had asked Jesus an intriguing question: 'Lord, will you at this time restore the kingdom to Israel?' Calvin comments that 'there are as many errors in this question as words'![3] It seems the disciples had things all wrong. Jesus' mission was not exclusively to Israel. It was much wider than that. He was going into *heaven*, not back into Jerusalem! He would be seated at the right hand of God, not in the upper room, or by the Sea of Galilee. He was going to exercise all authority in heaven and earth, not merely over the Jewish people.

Of course the Son of God always dwells in the presence of the Father.[4] He had never left his Father's presence in that sense. But now

---

[1] Acts 1:11.

[2] Acts 1:4. The 'promise' in view here is the promise of the gift of the Spirit of Christ at Pentecost.

[3] J. Calvin, *The Acts of the Apostles*, 1-13, trs. J. W. Fraser, W. J. G. McDonald, ed., D. W. and T. F. Torrance (Edinburgh: Oliver and Boyd, 1965), 29.

[4] John 1:18.

he was permanently departing *from his disciples* and returning to his Father in his human nature as the *incarnate, crucified, and risen* Son.

One of the staggering implications of what they were seeing was that the incarnation did not provide a merely temporary vehicle in which the Son of God was able to make a sacrifice for our sins. No – it was permanent, irreversible. Thus he did not jettison his body *en route* as it were to his original home, shedding it as if it were mere equipment needed for one era in his life, but not required in the future. This also implies that when he returns – as he promised, and as the two heavenly messengers now confirm – he will come again in the same way he left – visibly, physically, bodily. We are thus reassured that in the fullest sense 'Jesus Christ is the same yesterday and today and forever.'[1]

Identity

Jesus disappeared into a cloud.

We need to remember that these disciples had been old covenant believers – they lived and thought in what we would call Old Testament terms. And so, as we stand alongside them on Ascension Day we need to see the event through their spectacle lenses – and these were crafted according to an old covenant prescription. That means asking the question 'What does this cloud symbolize?'

We have seen this cloud before. When God came on Mount Sinai he came in a cloud of glory. He led his people through the wilderness by means of a pillar of fire by night that appeared as a cloud by day; when Moses met with God in the tent of meeting, the pillar of cloud stood at the entrance of the tent.[2] When the ark of the covenant was brought into the holy place in Solomon's temple the same cloud 'filled the house of the LORD' so that 'the priests could not stand to minister because of the cloud, for the glory of the LORD filled the house of the LORD'.[3] Was this what Isaiah also experienced in his heavenly vision when he saw the Lord and 'the house was filled with smoke'?[4] It was

---

[1] Hebrews 13:8.
[2] Exodus 13:21-22; 33:7-11.
[3] 1 Kings 8:10-11.
[4] Isaiah 6:4.

this cloud that had enshrouded Jesus, Peter, James and John just as Moses and Elijah were leaving them on the Mount of Transfiguration. This glory cloud which Jesus entered was real, but it was also symbolic. It was a symbol of the presence of the glory of God. It is therefore also an expression of Jesus' identity.

The message is clear enough: Jesus is going back now into the very presence of God. As Paul notes, 'he was received up into glory',[1] into the effulgence of God's presence. He has gone as the one who came to dwell with us in our flesh to where John said he was from all eternity – 'with God', 'towards God', 'face to face with God'. Into the depths of that communion we cannot probe; we can only stand and gaze 'lost in wonder, love, and praise'.[2] It is in this glory cloud that the eternal Son returns to the presence of the eternal Father. The entire scene marks out our Saviour as God the Son.

Victory

Jesus had triumphed. His enemies had engineered his crucifixion. It seemed to be a matter of callous indifference to them that in the process they had committed a catalogue of breaches of the ten commandments.

These enemies had also made sure his tomb would be sealed and guarded. But neither the written nor the living Word of God can be bound. He had risen from the dead.

At some moment, early in the morning of the third day, Jesus' state of humiliation came to an end and his exaltation began. On the cross and in the tomb he had defeated his and our enemies on their territory. Now, weeks later, his honour and dignity were being further advanced: he was riding in the glory cloud, as if on a victor's triumph. This was a new stage in the celebration of his finished work. He had become *Christus Victor*, Christ the Conqueror of sin, death, Satan, and all the forces of darkness. All this is expressed by a memorable physical event. The message is: Jesus is now ascending to his throne; Jesus is reigning. All authority in heaven and earth is now his.[3]

---

[1] 1 Timothy 3:16.
[2] The allusion is to the closing words of the hymn by Charles Wesley (1707–88), 'Love Divine, all loves excelling.'
[3] Matthew 28:18.

The ascension is about the kingship of Jesus. He has been in a prolonged and fierce battle. But he has proved victorious. He has dealt with sin, conquered the grave, and defeated the powers of darkness. And now he is mounting his throne. The angels, whose prince he is, wait to greet him. The glory cloud accompanies him as he makes his way in triumph to the throne.

Occasionally a victorious Roman general would be granted a 'triumph' – the equivalent in antiquity of a ticker-tape welcome. He would enter Rome, riding in a chariot, his spoils of war paraded before the adoring citizens. But the Romans did not lack an understanding of human *hubris*. A man could easily be carried away on such an occasion, and believe he was a god-like figure. And so a slave was stationed in his chariot to repeat two words to him, again and again: '*Homo es* – you are only a man!'

But this triumph is different. This is the triumph of the Divine Warrior. 'When he ascended on high', quotes Paul from Psalm 68:18, 'he led a host of captives.' This is 'the LORD, strong and mighty in battle'.[1] He is returning to his heavenly Father. The event is suffused with significance – for him and for us. For as John Flavel put it: 'If Christ had not ascended, how could we be sure that God did not have any more bills against us?'[2] But now all our debts have been paid. He has finished the work he came to do. Angels and men can sing:

> All his work is ended,
> Joyfully we sing;
> Jesus has ascended!
> Glory to our King![3]

We can scarcely begin to imagine the sight and the sounds of his reception into heaven: angels, archangels, cherubim, seraphim, elders, creatures that perhaps we know nothing about in God's realm of heaven welcoming their Lord – for they are the hosts of which he is the King of glory.

We often think of heaven as far away. But in fact in a manner we cannot quite grasp it sometimes seems to be very close. The ascension

---

[1] Ephesians 4:8; Psalm 24: 8.

[2] John Flavel, *The Works of John Flavel*, 6 volumes (reprinted London: Banner of Truth Trust, 1968), 1:508.

[3] The refrain from the hymn by Frances Ridley Havergal (1836–79) 'Golden harps are sounding.'

136

took place, as C. S. Lewis suggests, through something like a fold in space.[1] Heaven here seems like a parallel universe; it is close.

This is the homecoming of the Son of God. Perhaps you have experienced a homecoming yourself, or been part of one. Or perhaps you have seen video clips on television or YouTube – soldiers coming back from conflict zones and arriving at the airport. Family members are eagerly waiting. They have banners and balloons, and sometimes musicians. They stand on tiptoe to catch the first glimpse of their loved one. They are bursting with emotion, longing for the first sight of the long-absent face. As soon as they see their loved one they rush forward. It is a reunion. It is family time.

Now magnify that scene until all the ransomed host of heaven is visible in your mind's eye. See Christ surrounded by the angels of God. Feel the sheer glory of the moment. There is an explosion of praise: the Lord, strong and mighty in battle – the Son of the Father – the Crucified and Risen One – he has come home in triumph! Heaven itself is filled with a sense of joy and wonder that he has triumphed over the unimaginable onslaught of all the forces of darkness and evil.

Kingship

But more than being a sign of Christ's victory, the Ascension is a sign of his kingship.

At least some of those who first read Luke's account of the Ascension must have sensed that there was a subliminal message in it. This was, after all, the world of the Roman Empire.

After Julius Caesar died, and his body was cremated, a comet appeared that was taken as a sign of his deification. His successor was therefore the son of God. This became virtually the tradition – *Imperator Divinus*, the Divine Emperor – *Kaesar Kurios* – Caesar is Lord! Without actually stating it in so many words, Luke is underscoring that there is only one who has been raised from the dead and has ascended. *Christos Kurios,* Jesus Christ is Lord! He has ascended and now sits on a throne governing the universe.

If this is indeed what Luke implied at the beginning of the Acts of the Apostles, then it runs parallel to a hint that he had given at the beginning of his Gospel. On earth Caesar Augustus issued his decree

[1] See the extended discussion in C. S. Lewis, *Miracles* (New York: Simon & Schuster, 1996), 204-208.

that all the world should be registered to be brought under the tax jurisdiction of Rome. But in heaven God had issued another decree – that his Son would be sent to men and women of every tribe, people, and tongue, and that all the world should be registered to hear the good news of the gospel of Jesus Christ! The heralds of heaven had declared, 'For unto you is born this day in the city of David a Saviour who is *Christ the Lord*.'[1]

The sign *then* had been that he was 'wrapped ... in swaddling cloths and lying in a manger'.[2] The sign *now*? He enters heaven wrapped in the *Shekinah* glory of deity!

Here is how Simon Peter explained it all in his great sermon on the day of Pentecost:

> God raised him up, loosing the pangs of death because it was not possible for him to be held by it. For David says concerning him,
>
>> 'I saw the Lord always before me,
>>   for he is at my right hand that I may not be shaken;
>> therefore my heart was glad and my tongue rejoiced;
>>   my flesh also will dwell in hope.
>> For you will not abandon my soul to Hades,
>>   or let your Holy One see corruption.
>> You have made known to me the paths of life;
>>   you will make me full of gladness with your presence.'
>
> Brothers, I may say to you with confidence about the patriarch David that he both died and was buried, and his tomb is with us to this day. Being therefore a prophet and knowing that God had sworn with an oath to him that he would set one of his descendants on his throne, he foresaw and spoke about the resurrection of Christ, that he was not abandoned to Hades, nor did his flesh see corruption.[3]

Peter is explaining, step by step, what lies behind the Ascension. God has set his own Son on the throne!

---

[1] Luke 2:11.
[2] Luke 2:12.
[3] Acts 2:24-31. The quotation is from Psalm 16:8-11.

Psalm 24

Christians in the past saw Psalm 24 as a vivid foreshadowing of the Ascension. Christ Jesus is the one who ascends 'the hill of the Lord',[1] to approach the throne of heaven. As he returns in triumph the command is given:

> Lift up your heads, O gates!
> And be lifted up, O ancient doors,
> That the King of glory may come in.

But the question is asked:

> Who is this King of glory?

To which the resounding answer is given:

> The LORD, strong and mighty,
> The LORD, mighty in battle!
> Lift up your heads, O gates!
> And lift them up, O ancient doors,
> That the King of glory may come in.[2]

Have you caught this vision of the kingship of Jesus? He is no longer on a cross. He is no longer in a tomb. He is no longer on this earth. He sits enthroned at the right hand of the Majesty on high.

Intercession

But what does Jesus do there, as he sits at God's right hand?

He is holding the universe in the palms of his hands.

He is ordering every event and every detail of our lives in his providence.

And he is interceding for his people: 'He always lives', writes the author of Hebrews, 'to make intercession' for us.[3]

The Ascension of Christ is therefore one of the great articles of the Christian faith. It is embedded in the Apostles' Creed: 'He ascended into heaven and sits on the right hand of God the Father Almighty.'

'But', you may say, 'that is for Sunday. What about Monday morning? What about my practical life and my family, and my problems and trials? What relevance does this have?'

---

[1] Psalm 24:3.
[2] Psalm 24:7-10.
[3] Hebrews 7:25.

The truth is that our problems are far too great for us to deal with by ourselves. They will crush us. If that is not true of today, then one day – even if it is our last day, perhaps especially when it is our last day – it will be true of us. If life does not crush us now then death will. So we all need someone who will hold on to us; someone who will pray for us.

Now listen to Jesus speaking to his loving Father on your behalf:

> Father, look at what I have done for them. I died for him – and for her. I secured atonement for them. They are children of the King. Now, Father, show your love to them. Give them what they need. Bring them home; bring them all the way home.

It is a moving thing to hear someone else pray for you, isn't it? – to hear them address their Father and in their prayer to mention you by name. If someone who does that for you lives close to the Lord, you have a sense that they are being heard, don't you? But what Scripture is teaching us here goes far beyond that. None other than the ascended King of kings and Lord of lords intercedes for us. He does so on the basis of all that he has accomplished. And his Father always hears him![1]

Have you caught that vision? As John 'Rabbi' Duncan said, 'The Dust of the Earth is on the throne of the Majesty on High.'[2] Think of it, and draw comfort from it!

Pentecost

Death, Resurrection, Ascension … and then? Pentecost. These are all movements in the single symphony of Christ's saving work. As a result of his ascension Christ intercedes for his people. He had told the apostles what his first petition would be once his Father had glorified him. He would ask him to send his Spirit to his disciples.[3]

---

[1] John 11:42.

[2] John M. Brentnall, ed. *Just a Talker, The Sayings of Dr John Duncan* (Edinburgh: Banner of Truth Trust, 1997), 29. John Duncan (1796–1870) served as a minister first in Glasgow and for a short period from 1841 to 1843 in Budapest, before becoming Professor of Hebrew in the Free Church of Scotland College in Edinburgh. He was a man of unusual gifts, better known for his wise and often pithy sayings than for any literary output.

[3] John 14:16.

In the upper room Jesus had promised the apostles, 'I am going away, and I will come to you.'[1] But how did he come? He came by his Spirit. He sent his personal representative agent, whom he calls the Comforter or Strengthener, or Counsellor – the Paraclete, who is '*another* Helper', that is, another like Jesus himself. In fact, Jesus says explicitly, 'I will ask the Father, and he will give you another Helper, to be with you forever, even the Spirit of truth ... You know him, for he dwells with you and will be in you.'[2]

On the Day of Pentecost, the world seemingly had come to Jerusalem:

> Parthians and Medes and Elamites and residents of Mesopotamia, Judea and Cappadocia, Pontus and Asia, Phrygia and Pamphylia, Egypt and the parts of Libya belonging to Cyrene, and visitors from Rome, both Jews and proselytes, Cretans and Arabians ...[3]

It was like a mini-gathering of the nations, as Diaspora Jews gathered together in Jerusalem for the celebration of Pentecost. How appropriate that when the Spirit came citizens of the whole world heard about the reconciling work of Christ in their own language.[4] It was as if the events of the Tower of Babel had been reversed.

What possible explanation could there be?

The strange events of Pentecost evoked many questions in the minds of the crowds in Jerusalem. What did all this mean? Simon Peter gave a breathtaking answer to that question. He told the listening crowd that what they were witnessing was actually the evidence, the proof, of something that had happened beyond the reach of eyes and ears. This outpouring of the Spirit was the guarantee that Jesus had now ascended into the presence of the Father and had asked for the Spirit to be sent to the church. He really was at his Father's side; he really had kept his promise:

> Being therefore exalted at the right hand of God, and having received from the Father the promise of the Holy Spirit,

[1] John 14:28.
[2] John 14:16-17.
[3] Acts 2:9-11.
[4] Acts 2:8.

he has poured out this that you yourselves are hearing and seeing … Let all the house of Israel therefore know for certain that God has made him both Lord and Christ, this Jesus whom you crucified.[1]

Now the ancient covenant promise of Psalm 2:8 was being fulfilled:

> You are my Son;
>   today I have begotten you.
> Ask of me, and I will make the nations your heritage,
>   and the ends of the earth your possession.

This could only be effected through the convicting and converting power of the Holy Spirit, as Jesus had promised.[2] Peter's sermon paints a picture we can almost see. We can almost hear the Father saying to the ascended Son: 'You have done everything we agreed, my Son, everything I asked of you. You share my throne; the Spirit is yours to give!'

The Ascension therefore is the forerunner of Pentecost. And Pentecost is Christ's assurance to us that he has kept the promises he made in the upper room on the night of his betrayal. He has not forgotten us now that he is ascended.

What the disciples found so hard to understand a few weeks before, they are now enabled to grasp. Their fear was that Jesus would become distant, far removed from them. How could it possibly be to their 'advantage'[3] that Jesus was going to leave them? But now they are beginning to see it. Only his going from them, in his ascension, could lead to his coming to them, to indwell them, in the person and presence of the Holy Spirit!

The result is that – if we are believers – Christ's Spirit is present with us, indwelling us and carrying out his mission of making the things of Christ known to us, and distributing his gifts among us.[4]

This is the point Paul makes when he applies Psalm 68:18 to the Ascension. Like a newly-crowned monarch Christ distributes gifts to his children. He does so, as Paul says, ultimately,

---

[1] Acts 2:33-36.
[2] John 16:8-11.
[3] John 16:7.
[4] John 16:14-15.

to equip the saints for the work of ministry for building up the body of Christ, until we all attain to the unity of the faith and of the knowledge of the Son of God, to mature manhood, to the measure of the stature of the fullness of Christ.[1]

Because he has ascended and sends forth the gift-giving Holy Spirit, every believer, every member of the church is involved in the ministry of the Lord Jesus, as he builds his kingdom, and extends his rule and reign in the world.[2]

Return

Reflect one more time on the words of the two men clothed in white. They asked the disciples why they were standing gazing into heaven. Jesus really had gone from them. There was work to do! The disciples did not need to gaze in disappointment that they would never see Jesus again. No, said the men,

> This Jesus, who was taken up from you into heaven, will come in the same way as you saw him go into heaven.[3]

In other words, the nature of his going is a precursor of his returning. The words were a signal to the disciples that they should not be paralysed by the fact that he was no longer with them – for the Spirit would come. But it was also a signal that they should live the rest of their lives conscious that their Master would return, as he himself had promised. They should therefore live as those who looked for that day.

The return of Christ is the next great redemptive moment on the divine calendar. Whatever God may do between now and then does not form the horizon on which we are to fix our gaze. No, the Ascension teaches us to keep our eyes fixed heavenwards. To be looking not so much to 'signs of the times', or even to the end of our own lives, but rather to 'the future of the Lord'.[4] For the next great

[1] Ephesians 4:12-13.

[2] For a fuller exposition of Pentecost and its implications see: Sinclair B. Ferguson, *The Holy Spirit* (Nottingham: InterVarsity Press, 1997), 57-92.

[3] Acts 1:11.

[4] The expression is that of H. N. Ridderbos, *Paul: An Outline of his Theology*, tr. J. R. de Witt (Grand Rapids: Wm B. Eerdmans, 1975), 487-562.

event on God's calendar is the return of Jesus. We are called to focus on him!

Until then we have this mandate:

> Go therefore and make disciples of all nations, baptizing them in the name of the Father and of the Son and of the Holy Spirit, teaching them to observe all that I have commanded you. And behold, I am with you always, to the end of the age.[1]

Teaching others everything Jesus had taught them involved them preaching the gospel to others, including these words which summon believers in every age to take the gospel to all the nations.

Here then is our confession:

• We believe that he was conceived through the Holy Spirit and born of the Virgin Mary.

• We believe that he was baptized into our sins in the River Jordan.

• We believe that he was transfigured in the presence of Peter, James and John.

• We believe that he suffered under Pontius Pilate, was crucified, dead and buried.

• We believe that he rose again from the dead.

• We believe that he ascended into heaven and is seated at the right hand of the Father, reigning and interceding for us.

And further

• We believe that he will come again to judge the living and the dead.

[1] Matthew 28:19-20.

9. The Return – *Coming*

Who is He who comes from heaven
Ushers in the new creation?

> *'Tis the Lord! O wondrous story!*
> *'Tis the Lord! the King of glory!*
> *At His feet we humbly fall;*
> *Crown Him, Crown Him Lord of all.*

1 Thessalonians 4:13-18

But we do not want you to be uninformed, brothers, about those who are asleep, that you may not grieve as others do who have no hope. [14] For since we believe that Jesus died and rose again, even so, through Jesus, God will bring with him those who have fallen asleep. [15] For this we declare to you by a word from the Lord, that we who are alive, who are left until the coming of the Lord, will not precede those who have fallen asleep. [16] For the Lord himself will descend from heaven with a cry of command, with the voice of an archangel, and with the sound of the trumpet of God. And the dead in Christ will rise first. [17] Then we who are alive, who are left, will be caught up together with them in the clouds to meet the Lord in the air, and so we will always be with the Lord. [18] Therefore encourage one another with these words.

WE come now to the last of the great 'moments' in the ministry of Jesus Christ: Incarnation, Baptism, Temptation, Transfiguration Decision, Passion, Resurrection, Ascension – and now his Return. Each of them reveals something in particular about Jesus and his mission. Each of them has a profound significance for our Christian lives. That is certainly true of the Return of Christ. As John Trapp, the seventeenth-century minister, wrote: 'Pinned like a badge to the sleeve of every Christian is that he looks for and longs for the second coming of Christ.'[1]

It is doubtful if that is quite true today. It may have been true in the heady days of the seventeenth century, perhaps for a variety of reasons. But is it still true? Disagreement, not so much about the fact of the second coming itself, but about what may (or may not) precede it, or follow it, and questions about its timing – these are issues that Christians have disagreed about almost since the beginning. But all of this, sadly, has a tendency to divert attention from the central issue: Jesus Christ himself is returning in glory.

In this context there is something very refreshing about the language which the great Dutch New Testament scholar Herman Ridderbos gave to his study of 'The Last Things': 'The Future of the Lord'.[2] The second coming is about Christ himself.

In view of all these disagreements and debates, when we think about 'the last things' it is helpful to go back to 'the first things' – to go back to the basics, and to grasp the first principles. Only when we have these in place is it safe to think further. That is why a very helpful place to anchor our thinking is in Paul's discussion of the return of Christ in his first letter to the Thessalonians.

---

[1] John Trapp, *A Commentary or Exposition upon All the Books of the New Testament* (London: 1666), 1031.

[2] H. N. Ridderbos, *Paul: An Outline of his Theology*, tr. J. R. de Witt (Grand Rapids: Wm B. Eerdmans, 1975), 487–562.

The Thessalonian question

The presenting issue among the Thessalonian Christians to which Paul was responding was the situation of Christians who had died.

It seems likely that many of the church members expected that the promised return of Christ might take place within their lifetime. But then some of their fellow members had died. That seemed to challenge their convictions, and created a problem for them. Their concern was this: What happens to those who have died? Will they miss out on the blessing of the second coming?

So they certainly believed in the return of Christ; they looked forward to it. They longed to see Jesus for themselves. But would those believers who had now died lose their share in the blessing of Christ's return, since they would not be alive to see it for themselves?

The major part of Paul's response was intended to reassure these Christians. Those who have died will experience the blessing of the second coming just as fully as those who are alive. They will not miss out. There will be no 'second-class citizens' at Christ's return. For, argues Paul, when Jesus returns the first thing he will do will be to resurrect those who have died. Only then will those who are still alive be caught up together with Christ to meet him. Both living and deceased believers will share equally in that event and experience its extraordinary blessing.

Body and soul?

The Bible does not delve into great detail in discussing what exactly happens to a believer when he or she dies. We are given only glimpses (for example in the Book of Revelation, and in a number of other places).

One thing is made very clear. Scripture teaches that the souls of those who believe go immediately into the presence of Jesus: they 'depart' and are now 'with Christ' which is 'far better'.[1] What a comfort it is to know that Christians we have loved are now with the Lord Jesus, in his presence, enjoying his glory!

Yet there remains much about this 'intermediate state', as it is often called, that is not altogether clear to us.

Death diminishes us. God did not make us of 'two halves' as it were,

[1] Philippians 1:23.

body and soul joined by a heavenly glue, but nevertheless divisible. He created us as his image for life in two spheres, for the environment of earth but also for communion with the Lord of heaven. It is this unified person – what God created as one – that death so cruelly fractures. It should not really surprise us if we cannot fully understand this. After all, death is a contradiction of creation. It is in the most profound sense 'something that is, yet ought not to be'. It is the ultimate absurdity.

So we were not intended for body-less life. If we look forward to heaven simply as an escape from bodily, physical existence we have lost our biblical focus. We were made for bodily existence! Thus Paul says to the Corinthians that while we long for heaven, it is 'not that we would be unclothed, but that we would be further clothed'.[1]

Some have wondered if Paul's hints here that we may be given a kind of 'interim-body'.[2] But whether that is the case or not, the Scriptures teach us to think of life after death not as our final destiny but as a major step towards it. The final destiny is the resurrection of the body and the coming of a new heavens and earth suited to resurrection existence. In this sense the Christian has a very 'solid' hope!

But here, in 1 Thessalonians, Paul is making the fundamentals clear. And it is these that we must have in place before we try to grapple with anything in his letters which might fit Peter's description of being 'hard to understand'.[3]

Here, then, are seven first principles related to the return of Christ:

1. A single event

The return of Christ is one single event, not two. We should not even think of it as an event with two different stages to it.

This affirmation is made quite deliberately.

You may have seen one of those bumper stickers that suggests that if the driver in front suddenly disappears then 'the rapture' has

---

[1] 2 Corinthians 5:4.

[2] This would provide one explanation for John's words: 'I *saw* under the altar the *souls* of those who had been slain for the word of God ... they were each given a white robe and told to rest a little longer' (Revelation 6:9, 11).

[3] 2 Peter 3:16. Notice that Peter is not accusing Paul of being 'difficult' but simply recognizing the fact that he wrote about things that are in fact 'hard to understand'.

occurred. Jesus has come back and the saints have disappeared; they have been 'raptured'[1] – thus causing automobiles, buses, trains, and for that matter planes and ships to veer off the road, off the rails, crash to the earth, or sink in the sea. So powerful an influence has this view had, especially in the United States of America, that it was rumoured that certain airlines would not allow a plane to be flown with two Christians on the flight deck – as a precautionary measure.

In this view, Jesus may return at any moment. But he will not return 'all the way down' to earth. Rather his return is planned to take place in two distinct stages. The first is unannounced. He will come to rapture the saints. This could take place at any moment. It will have no precursors. He could return before you finish reading this book. Then, after an extended period of time, he will return finally.

But if Scripture predicts anything that must occur before Jesus comes, he cannot come at any moment; certainly not in the next ten seconds. And in fact Scripture does tell us what must happen before the Lord returns – for example, the gospel must be preached in all the world.[2]

Sometimes it is claimed that 'the gospel' Jesus had in view in these words was 'this gospel of the kingdom',[3] and that this is a distinct message from the present gospel of salvation. But, with respect we must demur. The gospel message is that the kingdom has already arrived in Jesus Christ, although it is not yet consummated (hence we continue to pray 'Your kingdom come'[4]). Christians are its citizens here and now. 'The gospel of the kingdom' is the only gospel there is.

Otherwise (as, remarkably, some Christians have felt constrained to believe), our Lord's Sermon on the Mount[5] was not fully applicable to those who first heard it, nor is it fully relevant to contemporary Christians. But no such distinctions of substance between 'the gospel' and 'this gospel of the kingdom' will stand up to biblical scrutiny.

---

[1] The term 'rapture' is derived from Paul's statement that believers who are still living when Christ returns will be 'caught up in the air' with him (1 Thessalonians 4:17).

[2] Matthew 24:14.

[3] Matthew 24:14.

[4] Matthew 6:10. Jesus' words need to be read in the context of the present possession of the kingdom by the poor in spirit and the persecuted, Matthew 5:3, 11.

[5] Matthew 5:1-7:29.

The gospel must therefore be proclaimed in all the world before Jesus returns. In some sense the Great Commission[1] will be fulfilled, for when the present stage of his redemption is completed there will be believers in 'every tribe and language and people and nation'.[2] If that is the case then – perhaps – he may yet return within our lifetime. But the idea of an 'any moment return' and certainly of an 'any moment rapture' is, by and large, a novelty traceable to influences in evangelicalism as recently as the nineteenth century.

It is particularly sad if this view – as has unfortunately been true – is associated with 'sign-gazing'.

In our teenage years we heard preachers turn the locusts of Revelation 9:3, 6 into Russian helicopters (complete with pictures of sinister-looking locust-like helicopters to prove the point). Again some advances in technology have been seen as simply the stepping-stones to the mark of the beast.[3] In recent years yet more individuals have been re-identified as the antichrist. But this is not the goal of biblical ministry, which has its aim 'love that issues from a pure heart and a good conscience and sincere faith'. 'Certain persons', notes Paul, 'by swerving from these, have wandered away into vain discussion.'[4] Sadly too often this litmus test of genuine biblical Christianity is failed, and faith in Christ and love for him are conspicuous by their absence.

No, the return of Christ is the

> One far-off divine event
> To which the whole creation moves.[5]

When he comes the last word will have been spoken.

Unpredictable

Nobody can predict the date when Jesus will return.

Throughout history people have made innumerable efforts to do this. Sometimes otherwise sober-minded Christians have attempted

[1] Matthew 28:18-20.

[2] Revelation 5:9.

[3] Revelation 19:20. It is a curiosity of this whole approach that while there is an insistence on a *literal* interpretation of Old Testament prophecy a symbolic interpretation is adopted in reading the Book of Revelation, *e.g.* locusts become helicopters, *etc.*

[4] 1 Timothy 1:6-7.

[5] The closing lines of the poem by Alfred, Lord Tennyson, 'In Memoriam.'

to do so. We need not question their sincerity, but we do need to stress the very last thing Jesus said to his disciples: 'It is not for you to know times or seasons.'[1] Rather they were to receive the Spirit to enable them to be witnesses to the nations. In other words, 'Do not focus on date-setting but on Christ-proclaiming!'

If you are a parent you can probably remember the occasion you left your children unattended for the first time. They had reassured you often enough: 'Oh please, can't we just stay by ourselves? We'll behave. We won't do anything bad. But please, no more baby-sitters. We're grown up now.'

Then, perhaps, a situation arose when there were no 'baby-sitters' available. As you left your children you laid down a list of rules – mostly negative. But the major rule was this: 'Under no circumstances – unless there is a fire in the house – *under no circumstances whatsoever answer the door and open it to anyone.*' This – the absolutely essential rule – you gave them as you left the house.

It was, surely, similar with Jesus. The last thing he said to his disciples was: 'It is not for you to know times or seasons. *No date-fixing!*' Yet what have Christians been doing ever since? Predicting the second coming of the Lord. But the Scriptures were not given to us as a kind of eschatological crossword puzzle to solve. Even – indeed *especially* – the Book of Revelation is intended to be a revelation *of Jesus Christ.*[2] We are to 'love the appearing *of him*',[3] not become obsessed with the date when it will happen, forgetting that our chief calling is to serve him here and now.

There may well be prophecies to be fulfilled before Christ returns. Many Bible students have held that the New Testament Christians expected a massive-scale conversion to Christ among the Jewish people. Paul does say that 'all Israel will be saved'.[4] But whether he is speaking about a specific event in history, or simply affirming that in God's electing mercy Jews (like himself) will respond to the summons of the gospel, in neither instance do his words enable us to predict with accuracy the day of Christ's return – that was not the purpose of his teaching.

[1] Acts 1:7.
[2] Revelation 1:1.
[3] 2 Timothy 4:8, rendered literally.
[4] Romans 11:26.

But if it is an unpredictable event – what implications does this have for us?

We should live our lives just as these Thessalonians and other New Testament Christians were urged to do. Paul by no means denied that the second coming could take place within his lifetime. At the end of his life he knew he would die beforehand. Yet even then his eyes were still fixed upon the horizon of Christ's return.[1] In the meantime, in the light of our Lord's return, our calling is to live 'lives of holiness and godliness'; to 'be diligent to be found by him without spot or blemish, and at peace', since 'everyone who thus hopes in him purifies himself as he is pure'.[2]

Whatever we are to think about the great tribulation, the battle of Armageddon, the appearance of the man of lawlessness, or the man of sin, or the antichrist,[3] we cannot predict, nor should we attempt to predict, when the Lord Jesus will return.

The best, and most biblical, course of action then is for us is to live – probably more than many of us do – in the light of the possibility that Jesus could come back within our lifetime.

One day there will be a generation of Christians who will not die. They will be caught up to meet the Lord in the air,[4] and they will be transformed into a new mode of existence in the new heavens and the new earth. Like Enoch and Elijah apparently they will never be conscious of dying – only of being changed.

We could belong to that generation. Let us live as if we do!

So let us be clear about this. The next great redemptive event is the second coming of our Lord Jesus Christ. In him we trust; to him we look in faith; for his return we wait with anticipation.

2. *Triumphant*

When Jesus comes he will return in triumph. He returned to heaven in a cloud; he will come again in a similar manner. He will 'descend from heaven with a *cry of command*'.[5] Paul's word here (*keleusma*) was

---

[1] 2 Timothy 4:6-8.
[2] 2 Peter 3:11, 14; 1 John 3:3.
[3] Revelation 7:14; 16:16; 2 Thessalonians 2:3; 1 John 2:18.
[4] 1 Thessalonians 4:17.
[5] 1 Thessalonians 4:16.

used of a ship's master commanding the banks of rowers on his vessel, or of a horseman driving his chariot forwards. It exudes authority.

Our Lord Jesus' first coming was marked by humility and lowliness. He came as an embryo in a virgin's womb, a baby in a manger. In him Isaiah's prophecies were fulfilled:

> He will not cry aloud or lift up his voice,
>   or make it heard in the street.[1]

> He was oppressed, and he was afflicted,
>   yet he opened not his mouth;
> like a lamb that is led to the slaughter,
>   and like a sheep that before its shearers is silent,
>   so he opened not his mouth.[2]

But when he comes the second time it will be in glorious majesty as the Lord of the hosts of heaven, the Master and Commander of all things. It will then be clear that to him alone belongs 'all authority in heaven and on earth'.[3]

Paul later told the Thessalonians that before the Day of the Lord came a figure would appear whom he calls 'the man of lawlessness' or 'the lawless one'.[4] For all his apparent resistance Christ will simply 'blow him away' like a leaf on the wind; for 'the Lord Jesus will kill [him] with the breath of his mouth and bring [him] to nothing by the appearance of his coming'.[5] Despite the fact that this figure's influence is effected 'by the activity of Satan with all power and false signs and wonders, and with all wicked deception',[6] it will take only the appearance of Christ for him to be utterly undone. For Jesus comes to declare his final victory, to assemble all his people to himself, and to usher in the new heavens and earth where they will dwell together. His every command will be effective, for his people will then be 'saved to sin no more'.[7]

What a day that will be!

[1] Isaiah 42:2. Cf. Matthew 12:18-21.

[2] Isaiah 53:7.

[3] Matthew 28:18.

[4] 2 Thessalonians 2:3, 8, 9.

[5] 2 Thessalonians 2:8.

[6] 2 Thessalonians 2:9-10.

[7] The allusion is to the hymn by William Cowper (1731–1800), 'There is a fountain filled with blood.'

3. Audible

The return of Christ will not take place in silence. In fact, sounds will fill the air. Nothing about Christ's coming will be secret. It will be publicly announced: 'The trumpet will sound.'[1]

No matter how large the orchestra, if there is a trumpet playing – even in a hundred-plus-member orchestra – you can always hear its soaring and penetrating notes. Think of Handel's *Messiah* and 'The trumpet shall sound.'

Paul describes this in a striking fashion. It is 'the last trumpet'.

In Scripture the trumpet was sounded in various contexts: the coming of God at Mount Sinai; the announcement of the 'Feast of Trumpets'; the proclamation of the Year of Jubilee, that marvellous twice-a-century year of homecoming, when all debts and all bondage came to an end.[2] In addition, in the Prophets the sound of the trumpet warned of impending judgment,[3] or was a summons to the people of God to assemble from the four corners of the earth,[4] and to proclaim that the Lord is coming.[5]

The trumpet was also the instrument that announced the cry to battle. The battle protocol in the Roman army involved a trumpet being sounded three times. At the sound of the *last* trumpet a herald stationed beside his commanding officer called out to the soldiers, asking if they were ready. To which the response was given: 'Ready indeed!'

The 'last trumpet' functions in all of these ways, as a cosmic marker, like the words that used to appear on the final page of a book: 'The End.' Then all the prophecies of Christ's reign will come to fulfilment. The trumpet sound will proclaim the beginning of an eternal jubilee, in which the Lord of glory will bring in the day of eternal joy. Then, truly and fully and visibly,

> Jesus shall reign where'er the sun
> Doth his successive journeys run;
> His kingdom stretch from shore to shore,
> Till moons shall wax and wane no more.

[1] 1 Corinthians 15:52.
[2] Exodus 19:19; 23:23; Leviticus 23:23-4; 25:8-55.
[3] Jeremiah 51:27.
[4] Isaiah 27:13.
[5] Zechariah 9:14.

Then, at last, will be fulfilled Paul's staggering affirmation that 'Where sin increased, grace abounded all the more':[1]

> Where He displays His healing power,
>   Death and the curse are known no more;
> In Him the tribes of Adam boast
>   More blessings than their father lost.[2]

4. Personal

Wherever the Bible speaks about the second coming its focus is on the Lord Jesus himself. It is 'the appearance *of him*'[3] – that is front and centre. Nor is this a 'spiritual return', or some vague sense of the 'spirit of Jesus living on in the hearts of his disciples'. No, it is the very same person who ascended who is coming: '*This Jesus* who was taken up from you into heaven, will come *in the same way as you saw him go into heaven.*'[4] Paul simply confirmed this when he wrote to the Thessalonians: 'The Lord *himself* will descend from heaven.'[5]

We have already underlined that Jesus' second coming will be in marked contrast to his first coming. Then hardly anyone knew about it: Mary and Joseph, Elizabeth and Zechariah, a few shepherds in Bethlehem, some wise men from the East, Simeon and Anna in the temple. It was largely *incognito*, 'veiled in flesh'. He came in lowliness, relative poverty, and then descended further into shame and humiliation. His only birth announcements were to shepherds and to remote scholars in the East. His only death notice was pinned to the Roman gibbet on which he was executed. No herald in splendid livery proclaimed him. Yes, angels did praise God for him but were heard only by marginalized members of society – field shepherds.

> He grew up before him like a young plant,
>   and like a root out of dry ground;
> he had no form or majesty that we
>   should look at him,
>   and no beauty that we should desire him.

---

[1] Romans 5:20.

[2] From the hymn by Isaac Watts (1674–1748), 'Jesus shall reign where'er the sun.' The hymn is, in turn, based on Psalm 72.

[3] 2 Timothy 4:8, literal translation.

[4] Acts 1:11.

[5] 1 Thessalonians 4:16.

> He was despised and rejected by men;
>   a man of sorrows, and acquainted with grief;
> and as one from whom men hide their faces
>   he was despised, and we esteemed him not.[1]

It will be very different when he returns. Then what was veiled will be fully revealed. Then the curtain that was partially drawn back at his transfiguration will be removed completely. When he comes in his glory and with the Father's angels, 'this same Jesus', this 'Jesus himself' will be seen and known as he truly is, in all of his majesty. This one – the eternal Son of the Father who became incarnate, was crucified and buried, rose and ascended, and now reigns, this person, the God-man forever incarnate – and no other – will come personally to reign in glory.

For this Christians have always longed – to see him as he is. One day we will.

5. Visible

A variety of 'secret rapture' or 'two-stage coming' views have been promulgated throughout history. Jehovah's Witnesses, as is well known, claimed in the past that Jesus came invisibly in 1914.

A very clear, simple, but quite decisive negation of all such views is found in the vocabulary the New Testament uses to describe the return of Christ. It is an 'appearing' or 'epiphany' (*epiphaneia*), an 'apocalypse' or 'revelation' (*apokalupsis*), a 'coming' (*parousia*). These terms all suggest visibility. This is explicitly stated in the Book of Revelation: 'Behold, he is coming in the clouds and every eye shall see him, even those who pierced him, and all tribes of the earth will wail on account of him.'[2]

'How can that possibly be?' we ask.

We simply do not know. But the more we get to know about the remarkable and complex nature of the cosmos in which we live, the more we should recognize that there are wonders far beyond our

---

[1] Isaiah 53:2-3.

[2] Revelation 1:7. By some interpreters of Revelation these words have been taken (with much of the entire book) to refer to the destruction of Jerusalem in A.D. 70 . But this has been a minority view, and not one adopted in these pages. For a fuller exposition see Derek W. H. Thomas, *Let's Study Revelation* (Edinburgh: Banner of Truth Trust, 2003).

imagination that will come to pass. But there is limited value in our trying to speculate. There is also a considerable risk that by doing so we will become fascinated by questions whose best and safest answer will be found only in the event itself.

No doubt when the great transformation takes place we will see the answer. But what we are assured of in the here-and-now is that nobody will miss it, whoever they are and wherever they might be. Nor will anyone be left in any doubt about the identity of the one who comes. Every eye will see him in this, the greatest visible event since the creation of the cosmos caused the morning stars to sing together and the sons of God to shout for joy![1]

6. Transforming

The return of Christ will cause a metamorphosis.

Our word 'metamorphosis' is derived from the verb used by Matthew and Mark to describe the transfiguration of Jesus on the mountain.[2] When the veil is finally drawn back and Christ appears in his transfigured glory those who are 'in Christ' will also be transformed into his likeness.[3] His gaze will cause a reflection of himself to become visible in his people. Already this transformation has begun in Christians, but as yet it is in a largely hidden fashion. The world does not yet recognize who Christians really are, says John. Yes, we are already children of God and co-heirs with Christ; but 'what we will be has not yet appeared'. However this we know: 'when he appears we shall be like him'.[4]

Paul agrees:

> I tell you this, brothers: flesh and blood cannot inherit the kingdom of God, nor does the perishable inherit the imperishable. Behold! I tell you a mystery. We shall not all sleep,[5] but we shall all be changed, in a moment, in the twinkling of an eye, at the last trumpet. For the trumpet

---

[1] Job 38:7.

[2] Matthew 17:2; Mark 9:2, *metamorphoō*.

[3] 2 Corinthians 3:18. The process that the Spirit has already begun in Christians will then be completed. Paul here also uses the verb *metamorphoō*.

[4] 1 John 3:1-2.

[5] *i.e.* die.

will sound, and the dead will be raised imperishable, and we shall be changed.[1]

All of this Paul will later explain to other churches. But it is summed up here already in his exposition of the first principles:

> For since we believe that Jesus died and rose again, even so, through Jesus, God will bring with him those who have fallen asleep ... Then we who are alive will be caught up together to meet the Lord in the air, and so we will always be with the Lord.[2]

Notice how marvellously he speaks of loved ones who have died in Christ: they have 'fallen asleep'. Paul is not saying that when a believer dies he or she enters a state of unconscious existence, what is sometimes called 'soul sleep'. No, rather – however hard and painful the last stages of the pilgrimage may have been – in the end death for the believer is like putting your head on the pillow and falling asleep. Or if we were to try to express all that Paul means – *falling awake* into the presence of Jesus. For the believer the process of dying may be a trial, a sore ordeal, a difficult stage in the journey to the celestial city. But Christ has drawn the sting of death.[3] Death itself has now been transformed into the gateway to life. We fall asleep as to the body, but as to the spirit we enter the very presence of Christ.

Yes, says Paul, our bodies are 'asleep'. They rest in the grave until their resurrection. But they are only 'asleep'. Christians share a secret that has been decoded by the resurrection of Christ. He will awaken our bodies. But more. He will not merely *resuscitate* them when he returns; he will *resurrect* them and transform them. No matter how disintegrated they may have become, he will regenerate these bodies marked by humiliation so that they will become like his body of glory.[4]

There was a glimpse of this future at the time of Jesus' crucifixion and resurrection. Matthew provides an enigmatic footnote commentary on their ultimate significance. Through Jesus' death and resurrection a series of events of a cosmic nature took place:

[1] 1 Corinthians 15:50-52.
[2] 1 Thessalonians 4:14, 17.
[3] 1 Corinthians 15:55-56.
[4] Philippians 3:21.

And Jesus cried out again with a loud voice and yielded up his spirit.

And behold, the curtain of the temple was torn in two, from top to bottom. And the earth shook, and the rocks were split. And many bodies of the saints who had fallen asleep were raised. And coming out of the tombs after his resurrection they went into the holy city and appeared to many.[1]

What can this mean? Matthew seems to be telling us that Christ's death and resurrection were not isolated incidents.

Elsewhere in the New Testament Jesus is called the *archēgos*[2] of our salvation – the person who is the first to forge a path and by doing so opens the way for others to follow. Says Paul,

> Since ... Jesus died and rose again, even so *through Jesus, God will bring with him those who have fallen asleep*.[3]

What Matthew was describing then was a little foretaste, a 'trailer' for the event that is still to come. But in addition notice Paul's logic. He argues from a *premise* ('*Since* Jesus died and rose again') to a *conclusion* ('*even so through Jesus* God will bring with him those who have fallen asleep'). What will happen to believers will happen not simply *after*, but *because of* what happened to Jesus. Because he rose, the resurrection of all those who belong to him has become inevitable. He will keep his promise: 'Because I live, you also will live.' He is the firstfruits – the guarantee of the final harvest.[4]

For Paul, Jesus Christ is the Second Man and the Last Adam. Just as sin and death have become ours because we are all united to Adam, so resurrection life and the metamorphosis to glory will be ours through faith because we are now united to the risen Christ.

What a day that will be! Our loved ones, and we ourselves if we die before the Lord's return – we who have served Christ and together loved and worshipped him and each other – will rise again and be with Christ and enter into this realm of the new heavens and the new earth. Some will not have died at the time Jesus returns. They will also be changed, and all of us will share the same reality together.

[1] Matthew 27:50-53.
[2] Acts 3: 15; 5:31; Hebrews 2:10; 12:2.
[3] 1 Thessalonians 4:14. Paul felt 'torn away from them'. 1 Thessalonians 2:17.
[4] John 14:19; 1 Corinthians 15:20, 23.

How marvellous it is that although we are brought to faith one by one, on different dates and in different times in history, we will all be transformed, glorified on the same day, at the same time! No Christian will be left out. None can arrive early; none will come late. 'We shall not all sleep, but *we shall all be changed, in a moment, in the twinkling of an eye.*'[1]

How long is 'the twinkling of an eye'? It will take that long (or short!) for Christ to rid our world of sin and its curse, pain and deformity, disease and death, sighing and tears. Eden will be restored. No, more than restored – completed and consummated, itself metamorphosed in glory, as Revelation pictures it:

> Then the angel showed me the river of the water of life, bright as crystal, flowing from the throne of God and of the Lamb through the middle of the street of the city [this is a garden-city!]; also, on either side of the river, the tree of life with its twelve kinds of fruit, yielding its fruit each month. The leaves of the tree [never mind the fruit of the tree!] were for the healing of the nations. No longer will there be anything accursed, but the throne of God and of the Lamb will be in it, and his servants will worship him. They will see his face, and his name will be on their foreheads. And night will be no more. They will need no light of lamp or sun, for the Lord God will be their light, and they will reign forever and ever.[2]

This is why, without question, the return of our Lord Jesus Christ will also be –

7. Joyful

Paul surely wanted to encourage joy in the hearts of the troubled Thessalonians to whom he had been able to minister for only a short time.[3] He is meeting a real pastoral need. The death of those we love brings much sadness. Death remains 'the last enemy to be destroyed'.[4] Still today it continues its destructive ways, bringing painful separation

---

[1] 1 Corinthians 15:51-52.
[2] Revelation 22:1-5.
[3] See Acts 17:1-10.
[4] 1 Corinthians 15:26.

from those we have loved in Christ (and we continue to love – do not forget that this too is a blessing of the gospel).

But Paul has some words of profound encouragement for his Christian friends. If they grasp what he is saying they will also be able to 'encourage one another with these words'.[1]

The joy which we have already tasted is to be ours without measure and without end in the presence of Christ. Hear the great English poet William Cowper:

> Dear dying Lamb, Thy precious blood
> Shall never lose its power,
> Till all the ransomed church of God
> Be saved to sin no more.
>
> Then in a nobler, sweeter song
> I'll sing Thy power to save,
> When this poor lisping, stammering tongue
> Lies silent in the grave.[2]

Cowper suffered profoundly from depression and on several occasions attempted to end his life. Humanly speaking he was preserved in large measure by his friendship with John Newton who, wisely, gave him work to do – together they composed an entire hymn-book![3]

Yet in a real sense – much as we love Cowper's hymns, including this one – its seven verses fall short of the full hope of the gospel. Perhaps Cowper's afflicted mind could scarcely take it in. Perhaps the horizon of eighteenth-century Christianity was not big enough to help him. For the gospel not only promises us freedom from sin and sickness in heaven. It promises us new resurrected life. Not only souls free from sin, but bodies, brains, minds, free from the effects of the Fall and of our own and others' sins. This is what awaited Cowper – and awaits every afflicted believer.

---

[1] 1 Thessalonians 4:18.

[2] From the hymn by William Cowper (1731–1800), 'There is a fountain filled with blood', originally entitled 'Praise for the Fountain opened.'

[3] Published as *The Olney Hymns* it contains three hundred and forty-eight hymns written by Newton and Cowper. It is included in vol. 2 of *The Works of John Newton* (Edinburgh: Banner of Truth Trust, 2015, new edition) 4 vols.

Does this not release a *measure* of real and lasting joy into our hearts now? And what will the *fullness* of that joy taste like then?

This world is not our ultimate home. We live too often as though it were. But in this world we are pilgrims, alien residents:

> Our citizenship is in heaven, and from it we await a Saviour, the Lord Jesus Christ, who will transform our lowly body to be like his glorious body, by the power that enables him even to subject all things to himself.[1]

Thus 'here we have no lasting city, but we seek the city that is to come' since, like Abraham we are 'looking forward to the city that has foundations, whose designer and builder is God'.[2]

When we read the New Testament from this point of view it dawns on us how significant the Lord's return is, and how it shapes the whole of the Christian life.

But we need help to keep this perspective.

God knows that. That is why the Lord's return is not only emphasized in the New Testament, but we are also reminded of it in the gift of the Lord's Supper.

The Lord's Supper looks back to Calvary and Christ's death:

> This is my body which is for you ... This cup is the new covenant in my blood. Do this, as often as you drink it, in remembrance of me.[3]

But at the table Christ also has communion with us in the present:

> The cup of blessing that we bless, is it not a participation in the blood of Christ? The bread that we break, is it not a participation in the body of Christ?[4]

We have opened a door to him, and he comes in to sup with us and we sup with him.[5] Forgiveness rooted in the past is coupled with communion experienced in the present.

---

[1] Philippians 3:20-21.

[2] Hebrews 13:14; 11:10.

[3] 1 Corinthians 11:25.

[4] 1 Corinthians 10:16. The term 'participation' translates the Greek word *koinōnia*, fellowship, communion (hence the Lord's Supper is often referred to as 'Communion').

[5] Revelation 3:20.

But there is a further dimension yet to the Supper:

> For as often as you eat this bread, and drink the cup, you proclaim the Lord's death *until he comes*.[1]

The Lord's Supper is a miniature drama. We celebrate it and enjoy all the blessings it brings to us. We feast on the bounty of Christ; together we enjoy our privileges; we are family together; we linger at the table. We wish it could last forever. But every time we come we are reminded that this is also a rehearsal dinner. The day is coming when our Lord will return and we will sit with him at the marriage supper of the Lamb. Thus whenever we come to the Lord's Supper our spiritual eyes are cleansed and our vision is sharpened. We see Calvary with greater clarity; we commune with the Saviour with deeper appreciation; and we rehearse for a day that is yet to come when Christ will return in majesty and glory.

One day we will sit down in a new heavens and a new earth. Here is the picture the New Testament gives us (the reality will no doubt be even greater than we can imagine): Jesus will take his place at the head of the table. He will sit down and reach for something to eat. All questions will be answered; all mysteries solved; all that is opaque will become clear. If there are lingering signs of tears because we cannot yet take it all in, he will wipe them away personally.

This is why we look forward to his return. For our Saviour, 'Jesus Christ is the same yesterday and today and forever.'[2]

Jesus is the same as he was 'yesterday' – the same one who came at Bethlehem, who was baptized at Jordan, who was transfigured on the mountain, who was crucified at Calvary, whose body lay motionless in death in the tomb, and who rose again and ascended in triumph.

Jesus is the same 'today' as he reigns in majesty.

And Jesus will still be the same 'tomorrow' when he comes in glory to consummate history, and to be with us for all eternity.

This *same* Jesus is coming again.

His return is the next grand event on the calendar of our salvation.

So do not be diverted, ever, from fixing your gaze on him. Look then for his coming, and live in anticipation of it. No, better, look for *him*, and live in anticipation of *him*.

[1] 1 Corinthians 11:26.
[2] Hebrews 13:8.

ICHTHUS

Who is He, in yonder stall,
At whose feet the shepherds fall?

'Tis the Lord! O wondrous story!
'Tis the Lord! the King of glory!
At His feet we humbly fall;
Crown Him, Crown Him Lord of all.

Who is He in Jordan's River
Takes our place as tho' a sinner?

'Tis the Lord! O wondrous story!
'Tis the Lord! the King of glory!
At His feet we humbly fall;
Crown Him, Crown Him Lord of all.

Who is He, in deep distress
Fasting in the wilderness?

'Tis the Lord! O wondrous story!
'Tis the Lord! the King of glory!
At His feet we humbly fall;
Crown Him, Crown Him Lord of all.

Who is He whose clothes now shine
On the mountain top He climbed?

'Tis the Lord! O wondrous story!
'Tis the Lord! the King of glory!
At His feet we humbly fall;
Crown Him, Crown Him Lord of all.

Lo! at midnight, who is He
Prays in dark Gethsemane?

'Tis the Lord! O wondrous story!
'Tis the Lord! the King of glory!
At His feet we humbly fall;
Crown Him, Crown Him Lord of all.

ICHTHUS

Who is He, on yonder tree,
Dies in grief and agony?

'Tis the Lord! O wondrous story!
'Tis the Lord! the King of glory!
At His feet we humbly fall;
Crown Him, Crown Him Lord of all.

Who is He, that from the grave
Comes to heal, and help, and save?

'Tis the Lord! O wondrous story!
'Tis the Lord! the King of glory!
At His feet we humbly fall;
Crown Him, Crown Him Lord of all.

Who is He that from His throne
Rules the world of light alone?

'Tis the Lord! O wondrous story!
'Tis the Lord! the King of glory!
At His feet we humbly fall;
Crown Him, Crown Him Lord of all.

Who is He who comes from heaven
Ushers in the new creation?

'Tis the Lord! O wondrous story!
'Tis the Lord! the King of glory!
At His feet we humbly fall;
Crown Him, Crown Him Lord of all.

Benjamin Russell Hanby
(1833–67; with alterations and additions)

SOME OTHER BOOKS PUBLISHED BY
THE BANNER OF TRUTH TRUST

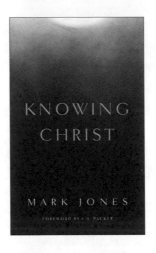

Knowing Christ
Mark Jones

272 pages | paperback | ISBN 978 1 84871 630 8

The Puritans loved the Bible, and dug into it in depth. Also, they loved the Lord Jesus, who is of course the Bible's focal figure; they circled round him, centred on him, studied minutely all that Scripture had to say about him, and constantly, conscientiously, exalted him in their preaching, praises, and prayers. Mark Jones, an established expert on many aspects of Puritan thought, also loves the Bible and its Christ, and the Puritans as expositors of both; and out of this triune love he has written a memorable unpacking of the truth about the Saviour according to the classic Reformed tradition, and the Puritans supremely. It is a book calculated to enrich our twenty-first-century souls, and one that it is an honour to introduce.

J. I. PACKER, from the Foreword

This is a work that will serve the church permanently in helping readers 'to know', whether much better or for the first time, 'the love of Christ that surpasses knowledge'. I commend it most highly.

RICHARD B. GAFFIN, JR.

Knowing Christ is a majestic gem that will be passed down from generation to generation as a beloved devotional. Its author takes the reader by a loving pastoral hand into depths and riches, exhorting us to know Christ better and to love him more.

ROSARIA BUTTERFIELD

Frederick S. Leahy

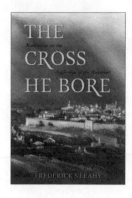

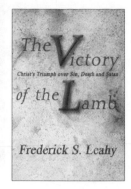

The Cross He Bore
Meditations on the Sufferings of the Redeemer
96 pages | paperback | ISBN 978 0 85151 693 6

Sometimes a book comes unhyped and unheralded and takes me by storm, and such is the case with *The Cross He Bore* by Frederick Leahy. Whenever I read it—and I have read it again and again—I am often compelled to stop and worship, to stop and meditate, or to stop and dry my eyes, thanking Christ for His immeasurable sacrifice. This little book is a true treasure. — TIM CHALLIES

Is It Nothing to You?
The Unchanging Significance of the Cross
132 pages | paperback | ISBN 978 0 85151 877 0

This wonderful little book of ten sermons … displays the Reformed faith at its absolute best, Christianity based on the Bible, centred on the Cross of the Lord Jesus Christ. — AUSTRALIAN PRESBYTERIAN

The Victory of the Lamb
Christ's Triumph over Sin, Death and Satan
144 pages | paperback | ISBN 978 0 85151 796 4

In eleven concise chapters the theme of victory is traced from Eden to the New Creation, highlighting the wonder of God's saving purpose which all the powers of Hell could not hinder. Throughout, the focus is on Christ as Saviour and Lord, conquering all the forces that held his people in bondage. — COVENANTER WITNESS

The Suffering Saviour
A Series of Devotional Meditations
F. W. Krummacher

464 pages | clothbound | ISBN 978 0 85151 856 5

First published in German in 1854 and reissued in English in 1856, F. W. Krummacher's *The Suffering Saviour* is a classic of nineteenth-century German pietism. In fifty-three meditations, Krummacher traces the last days of Christ from the announcement of his death to bewildered disciples through his sufferings in Gethsemane to Christ's internment in the grave and the eschatological hope of the resurrection. Krummacher's language, characteristic of the movement to which he belonged, is reverent and uplifting ... Of all the devotional manuals and chronicles of our Lord's life published in the nineteenth century, Krummacher's ranks among the finest and most popular.

RANDALL J. PEDERSON

Where can you find a book which so sweetly and solemnly sets forth the preciousness of Christ in His sin-atoning sufferings and death? ... The book is well produced, with good, clear print.

GOSPEL STANDARD

TWO DEVOTIONAL 'GEMS'

Jesus Himself
The Story of the Resurrection
Marcus L. Loane

144 pages | paperback | ISBN 978 0 85151 948 7

The believer's faith, love and hope would all be well-served by prayerful and meditative reading of this little volume. Unbelievers willing to read a book of this order would find themselves often face to face with Christ, and the enticing challenge of his person and work. In essence, it is full of the gospel, and the aroma of Jesus rises from it sweetly. To have your eyes turned to and fixed upon him, you could do much worse than to purchase and peruse this volume.

JEREMY WALKER

This is a choice little book, well suited to readers of every sort. It moved this reviewer several times to pause in the enjoyment of emotions which are out of this world.

MAURICE ROBERTS

This devotional study is a gem. The wonder of the resurrection is retold with heartfelt beauty. The strong binding, which resembles that of a presentation copy, is a perfect match to the contents.

JOHN M. BRENTNALL

The Loveliness of Christ
Samuel Rutherford

128 pages | Pocket Puritan Gift Edition | ISBN 978 0 85151 956 2

Surprising though it may seem in a world of large books, of all those owned by our family this may be the one we have most often lent or quoted to friends. It is full of rich spiritual wisdom and insight culled from the experience of a man who knew both the sorrows of life and the joys of faith in great abundance ... I pray that many readers will find here the help, comfort, wise counsel, and spiritual compass that we and our friends have so often discovered in meditating on these pages.

SINCLAIR B. FERGUSON

The Banner of Truth Trust originated in 1957 in London. The founders believed that much of the best literature of historic Christianity had been allowed to fall into oblivion and that, under God, its recovery could well lead not only to a strengthening of the church, but to true revival.

Inter-denominational in vision, this publishing work is now international, and our lists include a number of contemporary authors along with classics from the past. The translation of these books into many languages is encouraged.

A monthly magazine, *The Banner of Truth*, is also published. More information about this and all our publications can be found on our website or supplied by either of the offices below.

THE BANNER OF TRUTH TRUST

3 Murrayfield Road
Edinburgh, EH12 6EL
UK

PO Box 621, Carlisle,
Pennsylvania 17013,
USA

www.banneroftruth.org